ILE RPG FOR RPG/400 PROGRAMMERS

Robin Klima and
Richard Shaler

MIDRANGE COMPUTING

First Edition

June 1995

DISCLAIMER

Copyright © 1995 Midrange Computing
ISBN: 1-883884-14-4

Midrange Computing
5650 El Camino Real, Suite 225
Carlsbad, CA 92008

Table of Contents

List of Figures

List of Tables

Chapter 1

An Introduction to ILE RPG

The Integrated Language Environment (ILE) announced by IBM early in 1993 will forever change the way most programmers develop applications for the AS/400. Four languages are included in the new environment: ILE C/400, ILE RPG/400 (ILE RPG), ILE COBOL/400, and ILE CL. ILE C/400 was the first ILE language, introduced in V2R3 of OS/400. ILE RPG, ILE COBOL/400, and ILE CL became available later in V3R1.

ILE offers significant benefits to application development on the AS/400. Some of the most important benefits are a modular approach to programming, reduction in the overhead associated with calling programs, better control over resources, and better control over mixed-language interactions. Probably the most important benefit is that ILE provides a foundation for the future. The rapid increase in the use of object-oriented and visual programming methods demands a highly modularized approach to application development, which ILE supports. ILE RPG brings these benefits to the RPG programmer.

Before you can really exploit ILE RPG, you need to understand ILE concepts. This book starts by explaining these ILE concepts, then provides the details of coding ILE RPG. Many comparisons are drawn between the RPG/400 language and the new ILE RPG language to make the transition to the new format and syntax easier.

Here's what you'll learn in this book:

♦ ILE concepts to prepare you for coding in the new environment.

♦ How to convert your existing RPG/400 code into ILE RPG.

♦ The purpose and syntax of the ILE RPG specifications (the revised H-, F-, C-, I-, and O-specifications; and the new D-specification).

♦ How to perform powerful new operations on your data with built-in functions.

♦ How to perform date arithmetic and calculate date/time durations easily with the new RPG support for the date and time data types.

♦ How to locate programming errors quickly using the ILE source-level debugger.

♦ How to manage job resources better with the new ILE activation group.

♦ How to gain more control over exception/error handling in ILE RPG programs.

♦ How to access data efficiently through the ILE RPG pointer data type.

As a bonus, you'll also find a utility (written in ILE RPG) in Appendix A that indents ILE RPG source code on your screen or to your printer.

BENEFITS OF ILE

Modern application development relies heavily on the ability to combine small, reusable components—ILE provides significantly increased modular granularity. ILE's modular approach to application development also provides faster compile time, simplified maintenance, simplified testing, better use of programming resources, and easier migration of code from other platforms.

The scoping of resources can be better controlled through the ILE activation group construct. With ILE, you can create an application that runs independently of other applications within the same job. For example, a file override can be scoped to an inventory inquiry application without affecting an order-entry application that is running in the same job.

An important benefit of the new ILE program model is the ability to *bind* programs. To bind programs means to compile programs separately as nonexecutable modules that can be combined (bound together) to form a single, executable program object. Binding facilitates modularity and makes it possible to create reusable components without the performance penalty of external program calls.

Calls to a program that is bound to the calling program can execute with the speed of a subroutine. You no longer have to code the same subroutine into multiple programs because you are afraid of the performance hit associated with calling an external program. Programs written in one language can call programs written in a different language with consistent parameter passing, run-time services, and error handling.

A common source-level debugger services all ILE languages. Resources can be better controlled by partitioning a job into activation groups and controlling file opens, file sharing, and program loads within an activation group.

At first glance, ILE RPG might seem very different from the current version of RPG/400. After reading this book, you will understand why the changes were made and will have learned how the new ILE RPG makes programming easier and more efficient.

SUMMARY OF CHANGES

Significant changes have been made to RPG/400 to create ILE RPG/400. The most important new features that will make you more productive as a programmer, while increasing your ability to write high-quality code, are described below.

A source migration tool is provided to convert RPG III or RPG/400 source code to ILE RPG/400 source code.

The default source file name has changed from QRPGSRC to QRPGLESRC, and the record length has expanded from 92 to 112 bytes. The existing SEU date and sequence-number fields remain unchanged. The increase of the source statement length from 80 to 100 characters accommodates the longer file and field names as well as the comments in positions 81 to 100.

The new D-spec (Definition specification) defines what used to be defined on the E-spec and the I-spec. In fact, the E-spec has been eliminated from ILE RPG. Arrays and tables can be defined either as a stand-alone field (as they were defined in the E-spec) or directly as a subfield of a data structure. The D-spec is now the standard place to declare your fields, data structures, arrays, tables, named constants, and pointers.

One of the most frequent complaints about RPG is the six-character limit for field names. ILE RPG now supports 10-character file, format, field, constant, data-structure, key-list, subroutine, label, and other symbolic names. ILE RPG has generated some criticism because it only supports 10-character field names, while OS/400 supports longer field names. In fact, DDS directly supports only 10-character field names. Longer field names are supported only through the ALIAS keyword. For example, when defining DDS for a file, the field name EMP_NUM might have an ALIAS of EMPLOYEE_NUMBER. While ILE RPG does not support alias field names, it does support the full length of native field names for any file on the AS/400.

The underscore (_) is now valid in a symbolic name, but cannot be the first character. EMP_NAME is a valid field name, but _NAME is not.

Array subscripts are specified using parentheses () instead of a comma (,). ARR,X in RPG/400 becomes ARR(X) in ILE RPG.

Upper-/lowercase source is allowed. Upper- and lowercase characters can be used anywhere in an ILE RPG program. The field names EmpName and EmpLoc are now valid. The operation codes CHAIN, Chain, and chain all perform the same function. For example, the compiler converts the lowercase characters to uppercase. It is to your benefit to use mixed case for readability and program maintenance.

The compiler translates all source code—with a few exceptions—from lowercase characters (a to z) to uppercase characters (A to Z). Comments, literals (with the exception of hexadecimal literals), and compile-time array and table data are not translated. Also not translated are the currency symbol ($), date and time edit values on the Control specification (H-spec), date and time separator characters on the Input specification (I-spec), and comparison characters on Record Identification entries on I-specs.

Hexadecimal literals are translated, so coding x'f0' is the same as coding X'F0'. Compile listings show upper- and lowercase as entered by the user. The cross-reference listing appears in uppercase only.

The maximum length of named constants has increased from 256 to 1,024 characters. Numeric variables now support up to 30 decimal positions, up from 9. Character variables and array elements can now be up to 32,767 characters in length. This is a substantial improvement from the previous limitations of 256 for character fields and array/table elements.

The number of elements in an array or table has increased to 32,767 elements. The same goes for multiple-occurrence data structures, where the maximum is now 32,767 occurrences. Also, an unnamed data structure can be up to 9,999,999 characters in length. Finally, the length of compile-time table and array data has increased from 80 to 100 characters—the same length as the source specifications for ILE RPG.

Other limits also have been increased or virtually eliminated. The maximum record length of a program-described file has been increased from 9,999 to 99,999 bytes. Externally described files can have larger record lengths, depending on the type of system file. Also, the limit of 50 files per program has been removed.

Blank lines are now permitted. Source statements that are blank in positions 6 to 80 are treated as comments. An asterisk (*) in position 7 also forces a statement to be a comment just as it does in RPG/400. In general, positions 81 to 100 are treated as comments in source statements except for compile-time table and array data defined as longer than 80 characters.

Free-form math and logical expressions are available—with the EVAL operation you are now able to use natural mathematical expressions such as:

```
EVAL SLSTOT = SLSTOT + SLSAMT
```

Built-in functions are similar to operation codes in that they perform operations on data you specify. However, built-in functions can be embedded in expressions allowing you to code more naturally. For example, you can set a variable equal to a substring using the %SUBST built-in function within an expression as easy as this:

```
EVAL LSTNAME = %SUBST(FULLNAME: 16: 20)
```

You now have more powerful date manipulation capabilities through date, time, and time-stamp data type support.

Pointer support has been added. Now you are able to reference an area of memory by its address. However, performing pointer arithmetic is somewhat cumbersome. Run-time data allocation is not supported.

Many operation code names, such as LOKUP, DELET, UPDAT, UNLCK, and REDPE, have been changed to longer and more meaningful names (for example, LOOKUP, DELETE, UPDATE, UNLOCK, and READPE).

Now that we've reviewed the general changes ILE RPG brings, discover how to take advantage of this new compiler by examining the remaining chapters. There are many examples of how to use the new format and employ the new functions. Table 1.1 summarizes changes to the limits in RPG/400 that make up ILE RPG.

Table 1.1: Changes to RPG Limits with ILE RPG

Description of Changed Limit	RPG/400 Limit	ILE RPG Limit
Field name	6 characters	10 characters
Table and array name	6 characters	10 characters
File name	8 characters	10 characters
File record format name	8 characters	10 characters
Valid characters in symbolic name	A to Z, 0 to 9, $, #, and @	A to Z, 0 to 9, $, #, @, and _
Use of uppercase and lowercase	Uppercase	Upper- and lowercase
Length of character or graphic field and array element	256 characters	32,767 characters
Length of named nonnumeric constants	256 characters	1,024 characters
Number of decimal positions	9	30
Number of files	50	No practical limit
Number of arrays	200	No practical limit
Program size	Varies	No practical limit
Program-described file record length	9,999 bytes	99,999 bytes
Number of elements in table or array	9,999	32,767
Length of named data structure	9,999 bytes	32,767 bytes
Length of an unnamed data structure	9,999 bytes	9,999,999 bytes
Number of occurrences in a multiple-occurrence data structure	9,999	32,767
Length of compile-time table and array data	80 characters	100 characters

Chapter 2

ILE Concepts

Before you can really take advantage of the new ILE RPG language, you need to understand the concepts behind ILE. It is easy for you, as an RPG/400 programmer, to start using ILE RPG right away. For example, use the Convert RPG Source (CVTRPGSRC) command to convert your RPG III or RPG/400 source code to ILE RPG. However, until you understand the integrated language environment, you won't really be exploiting the power of ILE RPG. This chapter describes general ILE concepts that allow you to write ILE RPG programs the way they are meant to be written for the new environment.

WHAT IS ILE?

In February 1993, IBM announced a new model for programming languages on the AS/400—the Integrated Language Environment (ILE). As the name implies, ILE creates an integrated or common interface for programming languages. ILE provides the foundation for taking AS/400 application development into the future. ILE promises to enhance application development, quality, reliability, ease of maintenance, and performance.

But how does using ILE make all this possible? By examining the underlying concepts of ILE, you'll see how ILE brings all of these benefits to the table. But first, let's take a look at AS/400 language support, past and present. You will gain an understanding of how and why ILE evolved.

AS/400 Language Environments

Since the beginning of the AS/400, programmers created program objects from program source members. The number of source members varied depending on the complexity of the application and how many functions the programmer placed into a single program.

Original Program Model

Although many AS/400 programmers know about modular programming concepts and that creating small, single-function programs is a worthwhile design goal, this concept only takes the programmer so far. Smaller programs mean more programs calling other programs to run the application; calling programs adversely affects performance.

Before ILE, the only way an RPG programmer could call another program was to call it dynamically. This type of call is referred to as a *dynamic* or an *external* call. Dynamic calls require the system to resolve the reference to the called program before the program can be used. Resolving the reference and other functions performed at run time can be expensive as far as computer resources are concerned, resulting in degraded performance. The more program calls in an application, the more performance is affected. So, often a programmer combines numerous functions into one program to avoid too many calls to other programs.

The bottom line is that many programs on the AS/400 contain numerous functions and tend to be rather large. The longer an application is maintained, the more likely it is that the program has grown.

The environment just described, and the one that has been with us since the beginning of the AS/400, is known as the Original Program Model (OPM). It is the original architecture of the AS/400 (actually created back on the S/38). It works well as long as the application is not broken into modules.

However, the increased complexity of applications driven by graphical interfaces, event-driven programming, and client/server computing raises the issue of modularity. To simplify software development and maintain reliability, an application is broken down into smaller, reusable pieces. When working with these smaller, less complex components, the task of programming becomes easier—whether you're creating or maintaining programs.

Extended Program Model

For the AS/400 to remain a good application development platform it must accommodate a more modular design approach than is supported in the dynamic call environment. IBM actually attempted to provide better support for a modular environment when they introduced the Extended Program Model (EPM). The EPM was developed to support multiple-entry-point languages like C, Pascal, and FORTRAN. The EPM was supposed to allow applications written in modular-oriented languages, like C, to be ported to the AS/400. The EPM did allow for greater modularity. However, because the EPM operated above the machine interface, it created a much-too-expensive performance penalty. So, the EPM never fully accomplished what IBM had hoped it would.

ILE

ILE addresses the problems of both the OPM and the EPM by changing things from the ground floor up. Using ILE, the AS/400 accommodates increased modularity of applications. ILE not only encourages modular design, it allows a modular application to perform well.

Comparison of Program Characteristics

The characteristics of the three program models described (OPM, EPM, and ILE) are as follows:

♦ Original Program Model (OPM)

• RPG/400, COBOL/400, PL/I, CL, and BASIC

• Single entry point into a program

• Single scoping of variables (only global variables), except PL/I

- Access to data only through declared variables (no pointers), except PL/I

- Dynamic call binding

- Extended Program Model (EPM)

  - Pascal and EPM C/400

  - External procedure and function (multiple entry points)

  - Nested scoping of variables (global, local, block)

  - External variables

  - Static, automatic, and dynamic data allocation

- Integrated Language Environment (ILE)

  - ILE C/400, ILE RPG (RPG IV), ILE CL, ILE COBOL/400

  - Features similar to EPM, including the following:

    — Multiple external procedures or functions (multiple entry points)

    — Nested scoping of variables (global, local, block)

    — Access to data through variables and pointers

    — Static and automatic data

    — Dynamic storage allocation

  - Optimized code generation

  - Consistent exception model

Keep in mind that the functions of the OPM and the EPM are retained. ILE brings the best features of the OPM and the EPM into one evolutionary model at a lower level of the operating system. This allows traditional languages and new languages to work and to perform well together. You don't have to rewrite your applications under ILE. You migrate gradually to the ILE model.

PROGRAM BINDING

Now let's take a closer look at ILE and how it improves the performance of modular applications. One of the most significant features of the S/38 (predecessor of the AS/400) was the ability to call an external program from another program. This method encouraged the programmer to break down programs into smaller, easier-to-maintain pieces. However, it was soon discovered that you could only go so far with this modular design before the performance of an application deteriorated to an intolerable level. The reason for the performance decrease is the fact that external program calls are resolved at run time (dynamically).

In ILE, there is a new call mechanism, referred to as a *bound* call. The term bound comes from the fact that you combine (bind) two or more separately compiled source members into one program. To call any of the programs within the ILE program, you use the special bound call operation (CALLB). The significance of a bound call is its performance. With a bound call operation, the program is considered an internal procedure of the program, so the call is very fast without the overhead of a dynamic call.

A bound call has much better performance than an external call because it shifts the overhead of resolving the reference from run time to create time. The overhead occurs once, when the program is created, rather than every time the application runs. ILE RPG reduces the overhead of the RPG fixed-logic cycle when using a bound call. Only the parts of the cycle that are used are initialized.

With bound calls, you have the flexibility to structure applications in a modular format without having to pay a penalty in performance. The many benefits to modularity include better maintainability and well-tested, reusable parts.

Another benefit of modular programming is convenience among a team of programmers working on a single application. If you have a team of programmers and your application is only broken up into two or three parts, chances are the programmers are going to contend for the parts. This contention forces developers to make copies of parts, change the copies, and then dual-maintain the changes back into the original. This type of activity is error-prone and time-consuming. Using ILE, you can avoid this situation.

You still have the external call mechanism with ILE, and you can mix external calls with bound calls. This means you can start using bound calls gradually and where appropriate. Not all dynamic calls can be replaced with bound calls. For example, a call to an OPM program must be a dynamic call.

Modules

Now take a look at the anatomy of bound programs. As mentioned previously, with ILE you can combine programs so they behave as if they are one program. Here, combining programs means putting them together in a logical sense. In reality, ILE doesn't combine program objects. Instead, the system creates a new object type known as a *module*. A module is an intermediate representation of a program source member. Unlike a program object (*PGM), a module object (*MODULE) is *not* executable.

So, before you create an ILE program, first create a module. For example, to create an RPG module, use the Create RPG Module (CRTRPGMOD) command. To create an ILE CL module, use the Create CL Module (CRTCLMOD) command. In general, to create an ILE program module, use the CRTxxxMOD command, where xxx is the appropriate ILE language. When a module is created successfully, it can be used to create a program.

Programs

With ILE, you create a program with the Create Program (CRTPGM) command. Notice that the CRTPGM command doesn't qualify program with a type as with the old Create RPG Program (CRTRPGPGM) or the Create CL Program (CRTCLPGM) commands. An ILE program is not any particular type of program, it's just a program (object type *PGM).

An ILE program is made up of modules, which can be written in any ILE language (RPG, CL, C, or COBOL). Figure 2.1 illustrates an ILE program made up of three modules, each written in a different language.

Creating a program under ILE is a two-step process: create one or more modules, then create the program (CRTxxxMOD, then CRTPGM). Often, an ILE program is made up of only one module. If this is the case, create the program with the Create Bound xxx (CRTBNDxxx) command, where xxx is the type of source member used to create the program. For example, CRTBNDRPG is used to create an ILE program directly from an RPG source member, or CRTBNDCL is used to create an ILE program directly from a CL source member.

In Figure 2.1, the CRTPGM command places a physical copy of each of the modules into the ILE program. This is known as *bind by copy* or *static binding*. The term bind by copy is used because a physical copy of the module is made. The term static binding is used because the symbols between the modules are resolved at program creation time, forming a static link. (On some operating systems, this is known as linking.) If a module used by an ILE program is modified and recreated, the copy of the module that is part of the ILE program is not affected.

Figure 2.1: An ILE Program Composed of Three Modules

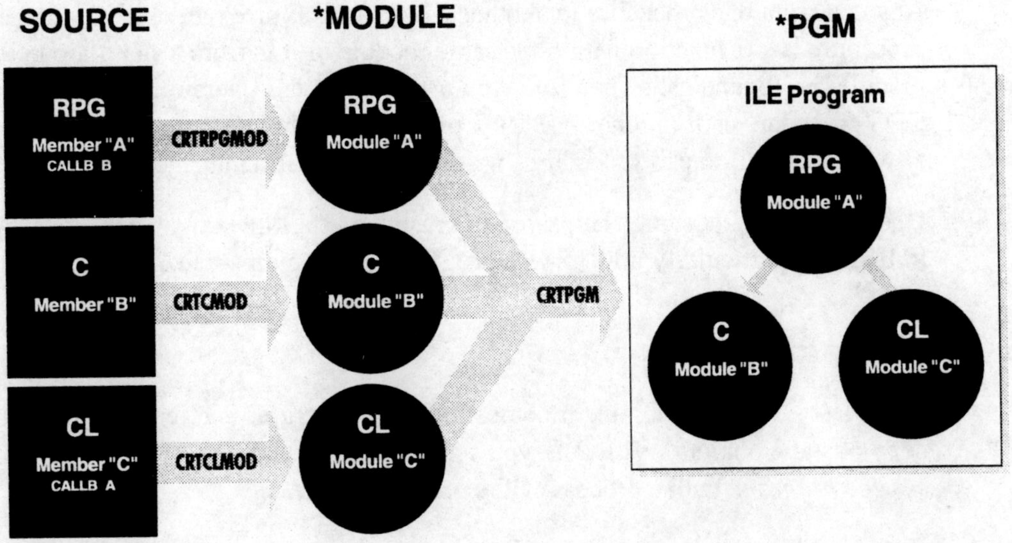

Let's say a module is used by many programs in your application. If each program has its own copy of the module and you modify the module, every program that uses the module needs to be recreated or updated. In an application of any size, this could become a maintenance nightmare. Also, all those copies of the same module on your system may not be the most efficient use of storage space.

There is a solution to this problem, and it is in a special type of ILE program known as a *service program*. However, before you can understand service programs, the concept of procedures must be understood.

Procedures

A more subtle concept than bound calls is a *procedure*, which defines a callable portion of code for ILE languages. In nontechnical terms, a procedure is a sequence of steps used to solve a problem. Generically, think of an ILE procedure as a set of high-level language (HLL) statements that performs a particular task. Technically, you need to make distinctions about how procedures are implemented in each HLL.

In ILE RPG, a procedure has a one-to-one correspondence with a module object. In other words, every module is turned into a procedure. In other languages, a module may contain multiple procedures. For example, ILE C equates the C concept of a function to the ILE procedure concept. An ILE C module can contain many procedures, and each one can be called independently.

Any call from one procedure to another within an ILE program object (whether the procedure is a C function within the same module or it is from a stand-alone RPG module) is a bound call. Therefore, you use the CALLB operation code when an ILE RPG procedure calls another ILE RPG procedure within the same program. You can also use CALLB to call procedures written in other ILE languages.

Understanding procedures helps you to grasp how multiple languages work together in ILE, and particularly how service programs are implemented.

Service Programs

In the last section, combining modules to create programs is referred to as bind by copy or static binding. With ILE, you can create a special type of program, called a *service program*, with a process called *bind by reference*.

Bind by reference allows you to call procedures with some of the flexibility and efficient memory utilization of a dynamic call. (The resolution occurs at program activation time.) This capability is made available through a call to a procedure in a service program. A service program (object type *SRVPGM) is similar to an ILE program in that it is an object created by binding one or more modules together. However, unlike a *PGM, you cannot call a *SRVPGM dynamically. You can only call the procedures within the service program. The only way to use a service program is to bind it by reference to an ILE program.

Creating a service program follows the same steps as creating an ILE program. Figure 2.2 is an example of two RPG source members against which you run the CRTRPGMOD command to create modules. After the modules are created, the Create Service Program (CRTSRVPGM) command is run against MY_MOD1 and MY_MOD2 to create the service program MY_SRV.

Figure 2.3 shows how to bind by reference the service program MY_SRV to program MY_PGM. The service program MY_SRV is bound by reference to the ILE program MY_PGM by specifying it on the BNDSRVPGM option of the CRTPGM command. (This option is not available with the CRTBNDxxx command.) Unlike a *MODULE object, which is copied into the final program object, only the information about the imported functions, data, and public interface in the service program is stored in the program MY_PGM. This allows you to have one physical copy of your code made into a service program and referred to by many different programs within your application, as illustrated in Figure 2.4.

Figure 2.2: Creating a Service Program

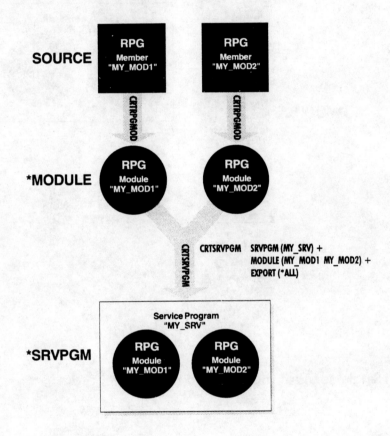

In this case, if there is a bug in the code used to create service program FRED, all that you would have to do is recreate service program FRED and replace it on your system. Programs ONE, TWO, and THREE, and service program JOE automatically pick up the corrected version of FRED. You are not required to rebind program ONE, TWO, or THREE, or service program JOE unless you change the exports (exports are discussed later in this chapter) from service program FRED.

Figure 2.3: Binding to a Service Program by Reference

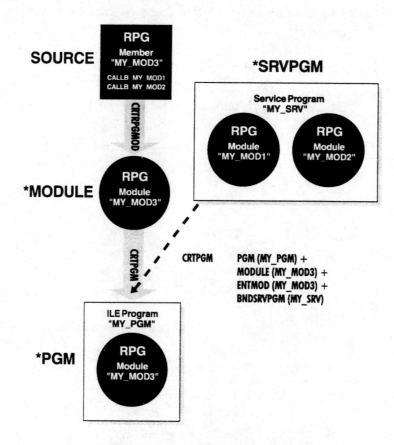

Figure 2.4: A Single-service Program Used by Many Programs

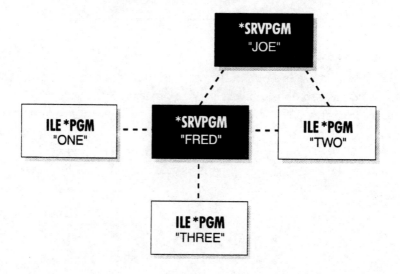

DESIGN CONSIDERATIONS

From a performance perspective, bind by reference is a little more expensive than bind by copy. The actual call using bind by reference versus bind by copy is virtually the same. However, when you call the program to which your service program is bound (activate your program), the exports are resolved. Thus, resolution only occurs once, at program activation, and not every time you call the procedures in your service program.

When designing your application, try to strike a balance between maintainability (which is usually easier if you use service programs) and application start-up performance. If you have a program that is bound by reference to a large number of service programs, there is going to be a noticeable activation-time penalty. However, once your program has been activated, any call to a procedure in a service program is a bound call, which is very fast.

From an application design perspective, there are many benefits to using service programs. One benefit is having a single copy of the executable code on the system (as illustrated in Figure 2.4). Another advantage is the ease with which you can maintain any code that is in a service program. Just replace the old service program with the new one, and the applications that call the service program use the new version without any recompilation. (Using dynamic calls to programs accomplishes the same ease of maintenance, but the performance overhead is much greater.)

Another advantage of using service programs within your application is the ability to control resources such as memory and file use. The ability to control these types of resources involves the concept of activation groups. Activation groups are discussed in Chapter 13. Suffice to say that data management resources can be scoped to activation groups, and a service program can run in its own activation group, depending on the parameters specified on the CRTSRVPGM command.

Scoping of resources defines how they are shared. A simple example is file overrides. Normally, the extent of a file override is to the call level, so that only programs running lower in the invocation stack of a job are affected. In ILE, file overrides can be isolated to activation groups so that programs running in one activation group of a job are not affected by file overrides created in another activation group within the same job. This gives application designers the flexibility to scope resources in any manner they choose, and still get the performance benefit of using bound calls.

IMPORTS AND EXPORTS

With any ILE module object, there are the concepts of *import* and *export*. An import is either data or procedures that are referred to in one module or program and defined in another module or program. An export is either data or procedures defined in a module or program and made available to other modules or programs. Thus, for every import there must be a corresponding export. Figure 2.5 illustrates how imports and exports work in ILE RPG.

Figure 2.5: Imports and Exports for a Simple RPG Program

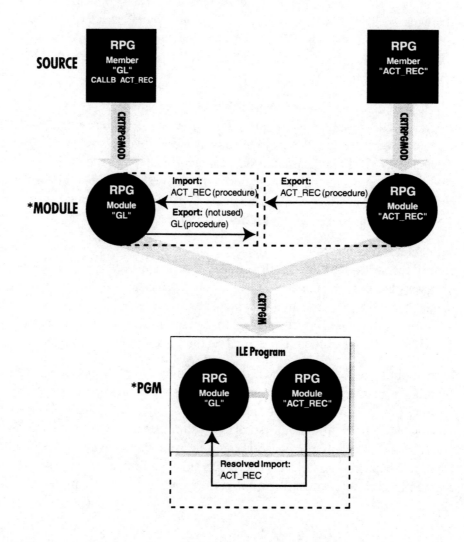

For C programmers, the concepts of import and export are well understood due to language constructs such as the external (*extern*) keyword and static data. For other languages, such as RPG, these concepts are not intrinsic to the language, although they are available in some of the enhancements made in the ILE languages.

The RPG source member GL has a bound call (CALLB) to procedure ACT_REC. Procedure ACT_REC is not defined in module GL, but it is referenced. So procedure ACT_REC is said to be imported in module GL. When you create module ACT_REC from source member ACT_REC, the procedure ACT_REC is available for use by other modules and is said to be exported from module ACT_REC.

During program creation, the import for procedure ACT_REC in module GL is resolved to the export of procedure ACT_REC in module ACT_REC. In other words, a matching export (procedure ACT_REC) is resolved for the import in GL.

For a simple bound call, such as the previous example, imports and exports are only concerned with resolving references to another procedure. However, imports and exports are critical to understanding how service programs work. As mentioned earlier, when you bind by reference to a service program, only the information about functions and external data is copied into the program object. This information defines the service program export information. Figure 2.6 illustrates how the export information from a service program is stored in the program object that is bound by reference to the service program.

Figure 2.6: Imports and Exports for a Program

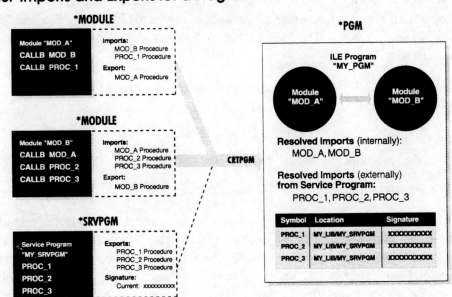

In this example, the imports MOD_A and MOD_B are resolved internally when modules MOD_A and MOD_B are bound together statically at compile time. The imports PROC_1, PROC_2, and PROC_3 are found in service program MY_SRVPGM, and the information about them is stored in program MY_PGM. When MY_PGM is called, MY_SRVPGM is activated. In other words, when MY_PGM is called, the exported procedures used from MY_SRVPGM are resolved.

The externally resolved import information is stored in the program object. If the service program that is resolved at run time has different exports than it did when it was created, you receive a signature-violation exception. A signature is a similar concept to a level check. It validates the public interface to your service programs. Every service program is given a signature unless you specify that you don't want one generated.

When the user of a *SRVPGM specifies the service program name on the CRTPGM command, the signature of the service program is copied into the program, as illustrated in Figure 2.6. When the program is activated for the first time, the signature stored in the *PGM is checked against the signature of the *SRVPGM. If the signatures differ, a signature-violation exception is raised.

SELECTIVE EXPORTING

The service program examples in this book presume that every procedure was exported from the *SRVPGM. A mechanism is available through a binder language that lets you specify which procedures and data you want to export from a service program. In essence, the binder language allows you to define a public interface to your service programs. The binder language is a simple language that follows CL syntax rules.

An example of the binder language that could be used when the service program in Figure 2.6 is created follows:

```
STRPGMEXP PGMLVL(*CURRENT) LVLCHK(*YES)
EXPORT SYMBOL('PROC_1')
EXPORT SYMBOL('PROC_2')
EXPORT SYMBOL('PROC_3')
ENDPGMEXP
```

The program level (PGMLVL) option allows you to specify multiple levels of exports that you wish to support. In this example, *CURRENT is specified to indicate that the current list of exports is used. The level check (LVLCHK) option allows you to specify whether or not you wish to have the system check the binding signatures. In this case, *YES is specified, which indicates that signature checking is enabled. The remainder of the binder language specifications list the exports for the service program. The binder language statements are executed by specifying EXPORT(*SRCFILE) on the CRTSRVPGM command.

Specifying an export list is the preferred method of specifying which procedures and data are to be exported from a service program. The other method is to specify EXPORT(*ALL) on the CRTSRVPGM command. This causes all external data and procedures to be exported from the service program.

Using a binder language specification is better than using EXPORT(*ALL) because the signature for the service program is generated based on the exports and the position of the exports. By using an export list, you have much better control of the signatures that are generated, and you have the ability to support multiple versions of exports.

BINDING DIRECTORY

If your ILE application consists of a large number of modules and service programs, specifying them on the CRTPGM and CRTSRVPGM commands becomes very tedious and error prone. There is a mechanism, called a *binding directory*, that solves this problem. A binding directory is a new system object of type *BNDDIR. Binding directories contain the names of modules and service programs that you may need when you create your ILE program or service program.

An important benefit of using a binding directory is that a module or service program will only be bound—either statically for a module or by reference for a *SRVPGM—into your program or service program if it provides an export that matches an unresolved import. The following commands are used with binding directories:

CRTBNDDIR	Create Binding Directory
DLTBNDDIR	Delete Binding Directory
ADDBNDDIRE	Add Binding Directory Entry
RMVBNDDIRE	Remove Binding Directory Entry
DSPBNDDIR	Display Binding Directory
WRKBNDDIR	Work with Binding Directory
WRKBNDDIRE	Work with Binding Directory Entry

The entries that you add to your binding directory need not exist on the system. They are only names that will be used later at program or service program creation time.

PUTTING IT ALL TOGETHER

There are two types of calls in ILE— dynamic calls and the much faster bound calls. Dynamic calls are external calls made to programs. Bound calls are calls made to procedures within an ILE program or to procedures in a service program.

ILE programs or service programs are created by binding modules and service programs. There are two types of binding—bind by copy (static binding) and bind by reference (dynamic binding). Bind by copy is the mechanism by which modules are physically copied into a program or service program object. Bind by reference is the mechanism by which information about the exports in a service program is stored in the program or service program object and is resolved during program activation.

You see some of the benefits derived from using ILE. However, binding is only one part of ILE; there are many other benefits.

SUMMARY

The following list summarizes the benefits of ILE.

♦   Better call performance. Under the OPM, external program calls can be expensive in terms of computer resources. The granularity of application program modules can only reach a certain point before application performance becomes unacceptable.

♦   Encourages modularity. Bound calls greatly improve call performance, so applications can be broken down into smaller pieces.

♦   Multiple-language integration. Use the right language for the job. Routines written in any ILE language can be bound to any other ILE module to form an AS/400 program. The fact that programmers can write in the language of their choice ensures the widest possible selection of routines. Routines written in any ILE language can be used by all AS/400 ILE compiler users.

♦   Software quality and dependability. When procedures are broken down into smaller, simpler functions, applications tend to be more reliable. There's no reason to create large programs that are difficult to understand and maintain.

◆ Ease of maintenance. Smaller programs are easier to maintain, and easier to understand. If they do need to be changed, a smaller program can be recreated much faster than a large program.

◆ Reusable components. Because modules can be linked to more than one program, the components of your application become reusable. You don't have to duplicate program coding efforts.

◆ Better control over application resources. The ILE environment provides activation groups, which can act as fire walls between different functions in your application. Activation groups help isolate functions at run time. If one function blows up, the fire wall protects the other components of the application from possible harm.

◆ Foundation for the future. Object-oriented programming (OOP) is one of the most talked-about subjects in software development today. One of the most important things you can do to ease the transition into an OOP environment is to break your application down into smaller, simpler pieces. ILE provides the ability to do this.

◆ Common run-time routines. Many application program interfaces (APIs) are provided as bindable (service) programs. For example, date manipulation, message handling, and math routines. Many more are on the way. Without ILE programs, you can not take advantage of these useful routines

◆ Consistent error and exception handling. An ILE program can register an exception handler and handle errors or exceptions in a predefined and consistent manner, no matter which language causes the condition to be raised. The exception can be made to percolate up the exception-handling chain until it is handled, even passing through activation group boundaries.

Chapter 3

Converting RPG/400 to ILE RPG

In this chapter you learn how to convert RPG/400 or RPG III source members to the new ILE RPG format. The conversion process is carried out through the use of the Convert RPG Source (CVTRPGSRC) command. The CVTRPGSRC tool converts RPG/400 source members of a specified source physical file to the ILE RPG format. You can convert a single member, generic members that match a specified prefix, or all members. The CVTRPGSRC command converts source member types RPG, RPT, SQLRPG, RPG38, RPT38, and blank.

CVTRPGSRC converts each source member on a line-by-line basis. After each member conversion, CVTRPGSRC updates a log file with the status of the conversion. By default, you also get a conversion report that includes information such as conversion errors, /COPY statements, CALL operations, and conversion status.

The conversion tool assumes that the RPG source code is free of any compile errors. If there are errors in the source code, some of the errors may not appear on the conversion report, and you won't be aware of them until you attempt to compile the converted source code.

PRELIMINARY STEPS

Before you run the CVTRPGSRC command, there are a few things you need to do.

♦ You must create a source physical file to receive the ILE RPG source members. The name IBM uses for ILE RPG source members is QRPGLESRC. The record length of QRPGLESRC should be at least 112 bytes long (12 bytes for the sequence number and date and 100 bytes for the ILE RPG statement).

♦ If you want an audit trail of the status of each member that is converted, you must create a log file before you begin. By default, the CVTRPGSRC command expects a log file to exist. You can ignore the log file by specifying *NONE in the log file (LOGFILE) parameter, but the effort to create the log file more than pays off if you run into any problems with your conversion. To create the log file, use the Create Duplicate Object (CRTDUPOBJ) command to copy the model log file QARNCVTLG in library QRPGLE to another library. The default name for the log file used by the CVTRPGSRC command is QRNCVTLG, so QRNCVTLG is a good choice for the name of the duplicate log file you create from the model file. You can create the log file with the following command:

```
CRTDUPOBJ OBJ(QARNCVTLG) +
          FROMLIB(QRPGLE) +
          OBJTYPE(*FILE) +
          TOLIB(your_target_library) +
          NEWOBJ(QRNCVTLG)
```

At the very minimum, the log file contains a record for each source member that is processed. You get a list of each source member compiled.

♦ If you use a data area for your RPG/400 control specification, you need to create a new data area in the ILE RPG format.

♦ You might want to make sure the source file containing your RPG/400 source members only contains RPG member types and no untyped (blank member type) source members. Because CVTRPGSRC attempts to convert source members with a blank member type, you could end up wasting time and cluttering up your audit log by having the CVTRPGSRC command process members that aren't really RPG source members.

Running the CVTRPGSRC Command

The CVTRPGSRC command should be submitted to batch, although you can run it interactively. By default, a conversion report is printed and a log file is created. Figure 3.1 illustrates the CVTRPGSRC command with all of its parameters. The parameters and their possible values follow.

Figure 3.1: The CVTRPGSRC Command

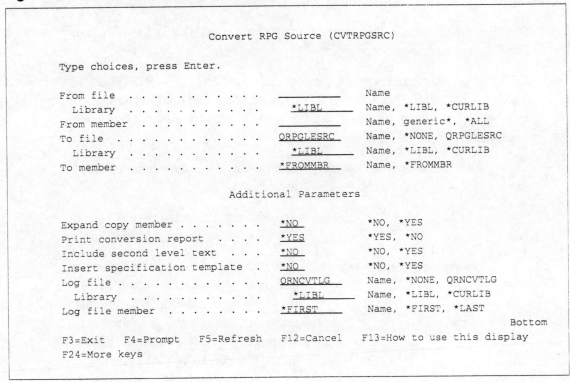

```
                     Convert RPG Source (CVTRPGSRC)

Type choices, press Enter.

From file . . . . . . . . . . .   _____   Name
  Library . . . . . . . . . .       *LIBL      Name, *LIBL, *CURLIB
From member . . . . . . . . . .   _____   Name, generic*, *ALL
To file . . . . . . . . . . . .   QRPGLESRC    Name, *NONE, QRPGLESRC
  Library . . . . . . . . . .       *LIBL      Name, *LIBL, *CURLIB
To member . . . . . . . . . . .   *FROMMBR     Name, *FROMMBR

                      Additional Parameters

Expand copy member . . . . . .     *NO         *NO, *YES
Print conversion report . . . .    *YES        *YES, *NO
Include second level text . . .    *NO         *NO, *YES
Insert specification template .    *NO         *NO, *YES
Log file . . . . . . . . . . .     QRNCVTLG    Name, *NONE, QRNCVTLG
  Library . . . . . . . . . .       *LIBL      Name, *LIBL, *CURLIB
Log file member . . . . . . .      *FIRST      Name, *FIRST, *LAST
                                                                Bottom
F3=Exit   F4=Prompt   F5=Refresh   F12=Cancel   F13=How to use this display
F24=More keys
```

FROMFILE

Specifies the name of the source file that contains the RPG III or RPG/400 source code to be converted and the library where the source file is stored. This is a required parameter; there is no default file name.

source-file-name	Enter the name of the source file that contains the source member(s) to be converted.
*LIBL	The system searches the library list to find the library where the source file is stored.

*CURLIB	The current library is used to find the source file. If you have not specified a current library, then the library QGPL is used.
library-name	Enter the name of the library where the source file is stored.

FROMMBR

Specifies the name(s) of the member(s) to be converted. This is a required parameter; there is no default member name.

The valid source member types to be converted are RPG, RPT, RPG38, RPT38, SQLRPG, and blank. The Convert RPG Source command does not support source member types RPG36, RPT36, and other non-RPG source member types (for example, CLP and TXT).

source-file-member-name	Enter the name of the source member to be converted.
*ALL	The command converts all the members in the source file specified.
generic*-member-name	Enter the generic name of members having the same prefix in their names followed by an asterisk. The command converts all the members of the appropriate type (for example, RPG and SQLRPG) having the generic name in the source file specified. For example, specifying FROMMBR(PR*) results in the conversion of all members with names that begin with PR.

TOFILE

Specifies the name of the source file that contains converted source members and the library where the converted source file is stored.

The converted source file must exist and should have a record length of 112 characters—12 for the sequence number and date, 80 for the code, and 20 for the comments.

QRPGLESRC	The default source file QRPGLESRC contains the converted source member(s).
*NONE	No converted member is generated. The TOMBR parameter value is ignored. CVTRPT(*YES) must also be specified or the conversion ends immediately.
	This feature allows you to find some potential problems without having to create the converted source member.
source-file-name	Enter the name of the converted source file that contains the converted source member(s).
	The TOFILE source file name must be different from the FROMFILE source file name if the TOFILE library name is the same as the FROMFILE library.
*LIBL	The system searches the library list to find the library where the converted source file is stored.
*CURLIB	The current library is used to find the converted source file. If you have not specified a current library, then the library QGPL is used.
library-name	Enter the name of the library where the converted source file is stored.

TOMBR

Specifies the name(s) of the converted source member(s) in the converted source file. If the value specified on the FROMMBR parameter is *ALL or generic*, then TOMBR must be equal to *FROMMBR.

*FROMMBR	The member name specified in the FROMMBR parameter is used as the converted source member name. If FROMMBR(*ALL) is specified, then all the source members in the

FROMFILE are converted. The converted source members have the same names as those of the original source members. If a generic name is specified in the FROMMBR parameter, then all the source members specified having the same prefix in their names are converted. The converted source members have the same names as those of the original generic source members.

source-file-member-name   Enter the name of the converted source member. If the member does not exist, it is created.

EXPCPY

Specifies whether or not /COPY member(s) is expanded into the converted source member. EXPCPY(*YES) should be specified only if you are having conversion problems pertaining to /COPY members.

Note: If the member is an auto-report member type (RPT or RPT38), EXPCPY(*YES) is assumed because the conversion utility calls CRTRPTPGM, to create an expanded source, prior to converting the source program.

   *NO   Do not expand the /COPY file member(s) into the converted source.

   *YES   Expand the /COPY file member(s) into the converted source.

CVTRPT

Specifies whether or not a conversion report is printed.

   *YES   The conversion report is printed.

   *NO   The conversion report is not printed.

SECLVL

Specifies whether or not second-level text is printed in the conversion report in the message summary section.

*NOSECLVL   Second-level message text is not printed in the conversion report.

*SECLVL   Second-level message text is printed in the conversion report.

INSRTPL

Specifies if the ILE RPG specification templates (H-, F-, D-, I-, C-, and O-specification templates) are inserted in the converted source member(s). The default value is *NO.

*NO   A specification template is not inserted in the converted source member.

*YES   A specification template is inserted in the converted source member. Each specification template is inserted at the beginning of the appropriate specification section.

LOGFILE

Specifies the name of the log file that is used to track the conversion information. Unless *NONE is specified, there must be a log file. The file must already exist, and it must be a physical data file. Create the log file by using the CRTDUPOBJ command with the From object file QARNCVTLG in library QRPGLE and the New object file QRNCVTLG in your library.

QRNCVTLG   The default log file QRNCVTLG is used to contain the conversion information.

*NONE   Conversion information is not written to a log file.

log-file-name   Enter the name of the log file that is to be used to track the conversion information.

*LIBL	The system searches the library list to find the library where the log file is stored.
library-name	Enter the name of the library where the log file is stored.

LOGMBR

Specifies the name of the log file member used to track conversion information. The new information is added to the existing data in the specified log file member.

If the log file contains no members, then a member having the same name as the log file is created.

<u>*FIRST</u>	The command uses the first member in the specified log file.
*LAST	The command uses the last member in the specified log file.
log-file-member-name	Enter the name of the log file member used to track conversion information.

The default values are fine for the most part, but consider changing both the Include Second-level Text (SECLVL) and the Insert Specification Template (INSRTPL) to *YES. Having the second-level text appear in your conversion report can save you a lot of time when you encounter errors. You probably won't be that familiar with the ILE RPG format, so having templates in your source members could be helpful.

Problems You May Encounter

Most RPG/400 source members should convert without a problem. If there is a problem, it will probably occur with RPG source members that contain /COPY statements. There are two types of /COPY-related problems—merging problems and context-sensitive problems.

Merging Problems

Because ILE RPG uses D-specs instead of I-specs to define data structures, programs that use the /COPY directive to include data structure definitions may not compile. For example, say RPG/400 program PGMA uses I-specs to rename some external file fields. Following the I-specs is a /COPY statement for source member DTASTRA, used to define a data structure. When compiled under RPG/400, the I-specs included through the /COPY directive are placed right after the I-specs used to rename the external file fields. There's no problem.

After running the conversion tool, source members PGMA and DTASTRA are both converted properly. But, when PGMA is compiled, the D-specs in DTASTRA are going to end up merged in after the I-specs. This causes a compile error because D-specs must be placed ahead of I-specs.

You can get around most of these types of problems by expanding the /COPY member. Specify *YES in the expand copy member (EXPCPY) parameter of the CVTRPGSRC command and the utility sequences the /COPY statements appropriately. However, you lose the source code reusability benefit of the /COPY statement with this method.

A better choice, even though it requires more work, is to correct the code manually by moving the position of the /COPY statement in your ILE RPG source member. As a general rule, if you use /COPY to include something other than C- or O-specs into your source program, you should plan to evaluate the log file and the conversion report closely.

Context-sensitive Problems

In RPG/400, there are times when it is impossible to determine the types of statements contained in a /COPY member without considering the context of the surrounding statements. There are two ways this can become a problem.

The first way is if an RPG/400 source member only contains source statements that describe data structure subfields or program-described file fields. The conversion tool won't know whether to convert the field to a stand-alone, D-spec data definition statement or to an I-spec definition containing a program-described file's field.

The second way is if an RPG/400 source member only contains source statements that rename an externally described data structure or that rename an externally described file field. The conversion tool won't know whether to create a D-spec for an externally described data structure or an I-spec to rename the externally described file's field.

In RPG/400, the L-spec and the Record Address File of the E-spec are changed to keywords (for example, RAFDATA, FORMLEN, and FORMOFL) on the ILE RPG F-spec. If the content of a /COPY member contains the L-spec or the Record Address File of the E-spec, but not the corresponding F-specs, the conversion tool doesn't know where to insert the keywords.

Unlike RPG/400, in ILE RPG you are not allowed to define a stand-alone array and a data structure subfield using the same name. Therefore, the conversion tool merges the array definition with the subfield definition. However, if the array and the data structure subfield are not in the same source member (one—or both—is in a /COPY member) this merging can not take place, and a compile-time error results.

If more than one RPG/400 compile-time array is defined and at least one of them is referenced as a data structure subfield, the loading of array data may be affected. To overcome this problem, the conversion tool links the data to its corresponding array through the **CTDATA specification. However, if the arrays and the data do not reside in the same source file (that is, one—or both—is in a /COPY member) the naming of compile-time data records using the **CTDATA format can not proceed properly. Figures 3.2 and 3.3 illustrate how the conversion tool handles a program where more than one array is defined, and at least one of the arrays is referenced as a subfield of a data structure.

Figure 3.2: RPG/400 Program Compile-time Array Referenced in a Data Structure

```
...+... 1 ...+... 2 ...+... 3 ...+... 4 ...+... 5 ...+... 6 ...+... 7
      E                   AR1    10   10  1
      E                   AR2    10   10  1
      IDTASTR     DS
      I                                      1  10 NAME
      I                                     11  20 AR1
**
1111111111
**
2222222222
...+... 1 ...+... 2 ...+... 3 ...+... 4 ...+... 5 ...+... 6 ...+... 7
```

Figure 3.3: Compile-time Array After Conversion to ILE RPG

```
...+... 1 ...+... 2 ...+... 3 ...+... 4 ...+... 5 ...+... 6 ...+... 7
.....D*ame++++++++++ETDsFrom+++To/L+++IDc.Keywords++++++++++++++++++++
      D AR2          S              1    DIM(10) CTDATA PERRCD(10)
      D DTASTR       DS
      D  NAME                 1     10
      D  AR1                 11     20
      D                                   DIM(10) CTDATA PERRCD(10)
**CTDATA AR1
1111111111
**CTDATA AR2
2222222222
...+... 1 ...+... 2 ...+... 3 ...+... 4 ...+... 5 ...+... 6 ...+... 7
```

Features Not Supported by ILE RPG

The auto-report function, the FREE operation code, and the DEBUG operation code are not supported in ILE RPG.

When CVTRPGSRC detects an auto-report source member (member type RPT or RPT38), the Create Report Program (CRTRPTPGM) command is called to expand the source code before the conversion takes place. Errors encountered during the auto-report expansion are not found in the conversion report; therefore, you may need to examine the spool file generated by the auto-report expansion to find the error.

Any FREE or DEBUG operation codes are listed in the conversion report. You have to remove these operations before you can successfully compile the ILE RPG source member. The conversion tool converts FREE or DEBUG statements to the ILE RPG format even though they aren't valid operations.

Although the conversion program converts from RPG/400 to ILE RPG, it does not include enhanced operation codes. It does not change arithmetic operation codes to EVAL operation codes. The conversion process is only the first step. You must take the next step—if you want to enhance it into more readable code and use bound calls to speed up your program—to learn how to program in the ILE RPG language.

Summary

The CVTRPGSRC tool is by no means the most exciting part of ILE RPG, but it is probably the first step that many will take when they enter the new world of ILE. The conversion tool should convert a high percentage of your RPG/400 source code without a hitch. If you do encounter problems, it will most likely be with source members that use the /COPY directive. At the very worst, you may have to modify some of the converted source manually.

Chapter 4

Control Specification (H-spec)

In ILE RPG, as in RPG/400, the Control specification (H-spec) provides information about generating and running programs. Instead of entering values in specific positions as you would in RPG/400, ILE RPG uses keyword notation. Figure 4.1 shows the general format of an ILE RPG Control specification.

Figure 4.1: Control Specification Format

```
 *. 1 ...+... 2 ...+... 3 ...+... 4 ...+... 5 ...+... 6 ...+... 7 ...+... 8
HKeywords+++++++++++++++++++++++++++++++++++++++++++++++++++++++++++++++++++
```

Positions 7 through 80 are used when entering Control specification keywords. This keyword notation is very similar to CL keyword notation: you specify a keyword, then optionally follow it by one or more values within parentheses. For example, DEBUG(*YES) is a valid keyword on an ILE RPG H-spec. It is the equivalent of placing a 1 in position 15 of an H-spec in an RPG/400 program to allow the use of the DUMP operation. In this case, you can see that the ILE RPG method is much more descriptive.

IMPLEMENTATION

The H-spec is optional in ILE RPG just as it is in RPG/400. You can decide whether or not you want to use it. If you decide to use an H-spec in your program, there are three ways to implement it:

♦   Enter the H-spec into the source member.

♦   Create a data area called RPGLEHSPC in your library list.

♦   Create a data area called DFTLEHSPEC in library QRPGLE.

The ILE RPG compiler searches for control information, in the order shown, until found. If not found, then default keyword values are assigned for the control information.

An H-spec in ILE RPG contains only keywords and their associated parameters. These keywords can appear anywhere in positions 7 through 80. Positions 81 through 100 can contain comments. Within positions 7 through 80, the keywords can be placed in any order or position as long as there is at least one space between each keyword.

Unlike RPG/400, an ILE RPG program can contain multiple H-specs. Each additional H-spec is considered a continuation of the first.

If you use a data area to contain the control information, then you need to create the data area as type *CHAR. When you specify the value for the data area, include the H in position 6. Only place the keywords that you want to appear in positions 7 through 80 into the data area. The data area can be any size as long as it's large enough to hold the keywords.

EXAMPLE H-SPEC

Figures 4.2 and 4.3 illustrate the difference between an RPG/400 H-spec and an equivalent ILE RPG H-spec. Both H-specs change the format of UDATE to Month/Day/Year. They also change the default separator character to a forward slash (/). The resulting format for UDATE is MM/DD/YY.

Figure 4.2: RPG/400 H-spec

```
*. 1 ...+... 2 ...+... 3 ...+... 4 ...+... 5 ...+... 6 ...+... 7
H       1 $M D     S           1 F
```

Figure 4.3: ILE RPG H-spec

```
*. 1 ...+... 2 ...+... 3 ...+... 4 ...+... 5 ...+... 6 ...+... 7 ...+... 8
H DEBUG(*YES) CURSYM('$') DATEDIT(*MDY) DECEDIT('.') ALTSEQ(*SRC)
H FORMSALIGN(*YES) FTRANS(*SRC) DFTNAME(ILERPG) DATFMT(*MDY/)
H TIMFMT(*ISO)
```

Instead of specifying a 1 in position 15 of the RPG/400 H-spec, the keyword DEBUG is used to enable the DUMP operation code. The use of DEBUG or DEBUG(*YES) enables DUMP operations. Not specifying the DEBUG keyword at all, or specifying DEBUG(*NO), disables DUMP operations.

The currency symbol in position 18 of the RPG/400 H-spec is specified using the CURSYM keyword with a single character enclosed in single quotes (''). If CURSYM is not specified, the currency symbol default, $, is used.

The date format and date edit characters in positions 19 and 20 are replaced in Figure 4.3 with the DATEDIT keyword to specify the order of month, day, and year of UDATE and *DATE, as well as the separator character for the Y edit code. The *MDY, *DMY, and *YMD formats can be specified.

An optional separator character for *DMY, *YMD, and *MDY format dates may be specified. The separator character is added to the date format. For example, specifying DATEDIT(*MDY.) causes dates to appear as MM.DD.YY when the Y edit code is used.

The DECEDIT keyword replaces the decimal notation in position 21 of Figure 4.2.

Alternate collating sequence is now specified with the ALTSEQ keyword instead of an S in position 26.

The FORMSALIGN parameter replaces the 1 in position 41 to request first page forms alignment. FORMSALIGN and FORMSALIGN(*YES) enable first page forms alignment. Not specifying the FORMSALIGN keyword, or specifying FORMSALIGN(*NO), disables first page forms alignment.

A file translation table is indicated using the FTRANS keyword instead of the F in position 43.

The transparency check in position 57 is no longer required.

The default program name is now specified using the DFTNAME keyword instead of using positions 75 through 80. If DFTNAME is not specified, or if the specified name is invalid, RPGPGM is used as the default program name. At compile time, a program name is usually specified as the same name as the source member, so DFTNAME does not need to be specified in most cases.

The DATFMT keyword is used to indicate the format and separator for date literals, which are required to support the new date data type. *MDY, *DMY, and *YMD support the traditional, eight-character (MM/DD/YY, DD/MM/YY, and YY/MM/DD) date formats. A number of other formats are supported also.

The TIMFMT keyword is used to indicate the format and separator for time literals, which are used to support the new time data types.

CONTROL SPECIFICATION KEYWORDS

As mentioned earlier, all values on the H-spec are entered in keyword notation. Table 4.1 shows the differences between RPG/400 and ILE RPG H-specs.

Table 4.1: Differences between H-specs in RPG/400 and ILE RPG

RPG/400 Position	Description	ILE RPG Keyword
15	Debug	DEBUG
18	Currency symbol	CURSYM
19	Date format	DATEDIT
20	Date edit	DATEDIT
21	Decimal edit	DECEDIT
New	Date literals format	DATFMT
New	Time literals format	TIMFMT
26	Alternate collating sequence	ALTSEQ
41	First page forms alignment	FORMSALIGN
43	File translation	FTRANS

RPG/400 Position	Description	ILE RPG Keyword
57	Transparency check	No longer needed
75 through 80	Default program name	DFTNAME
New	Date field format	DATFMT
New	Time field format	TIMFMT

The following section lists each Control specification keyword alphabetically and describes its associated parameters. Examples of how each keyword is used are included.

ALTSEQ (Alternate Collating Sequence)

Specifies an alternate collating sequence. If the ALTSEQ keyword is not specified, or it is specified with the *NONE parameter, then the normal collating sequence is used.

The possible ALTSEQ keyword parameter values are:

<u>*NONE:</u>   Use the normal collating sequence.

***SRC:**   Use the alternate collating sequence table specified in the program.

***EXT:**   Use the alternate collating sequence table specified in the SRTSEQ parameter of the Create RPG Module (CRTRPGMOD) command or the Create Bound RPG Program (CRTBNDRPG) command.

The H-spec in Figure 4.4 uses the alternate collating sequence table that would be specified in the program.

Figure 4.4: ALTSEQ Keyword Example

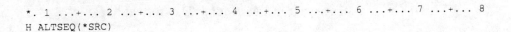

```
*. 1 ...+... 2 ...+... 3 ...+... 4 ...+... 5 ...+... 6 ...+... 7 ...+... 8
H ALTSEQ(*SRC)
```

CURSYM (Currency Symbol)

Specifies the character used as the currency symbol in editing. If the CURSYM keyword is not specified, then the dollar sign currency symbol is used. If the CURSYM keyword is specified, then it must be followed by the currency symbol parameter in single quotes.

The possible currency-symbol-character (CURSYM) keyword parameter values are specified by any single character enclosed in single quotes except '0' (zero), '*' (asterisk), ',' (comma), '&' (ampersand), '.' (period), '-' (hyphen), 'C', 'R', or ' ' (blank).

The H-spec in Figure 4.5 overrides the default currency symbol of a dollar sign to a pound sign (#).

Figure 4.5: CURSYM Keyword Example

```
*. 1 ...+... 2 ...+... 3 ...+... 4 ...+... 5 ...+... 6 ...+... 7 ...+... 8
H CURSYM('#')
```

DATEDIT (Date Edit)

Specifies the format of numeric fields when the Y edit is used. This keyword accepts two parameters. The first one is required, the second is optional. The first parameter specifies the date format, and the second parameter specifies the separator character. If the DATEDIT keyword is not specified, then the default date format is *MDY and the default separator character is a forward slash. If the DATEDIT keyword is specified, then it must be followed by a date format.

The possible values for the first parameter of the DATEDIT keyword are:

*MDY:	Dates appear in Month/Day/Year format (MM/DD/YY).
*DMY:	Dates appear in Day/Month/Year format (DD/MM/YY).
*YMD:	Dates appear in Year/Month/Day format (YY/MM/DD).

The second parameter of the DATEDIT keyword can be any single character. The default separator is forward slash. A separator character of ampersand appears as a blank separator.

The H-spec in Figure 4.6 overrides the format of the Y edit code from *MDY to
*YMD, and overrides the default separator character from a forward slash to a hyphen.

Figure 4.6: DATEDIT Keyword Example

```
*. 1 ...+... 2 ...+... 3 ...+... 4 ...+... 5 ...+... 6 ...+... 7 ...+... 8
H DATEDIT(*YMD-)
```

DATFMT (Date Format)

Specifies the format of date literals and date fields within the program. This keyword
accepts two parameters. The first one is required, the second is optional. The first
parameter specifies the date format and the second parameter specifies the separator
character. If the DATFMT keyword is not specified, then the default date format is
*ISO and the default separator character is a hyphen. If the DATFMT keyword is
specified, then it must be followed by a date format.

The possible values for the first parameter of the DATFMT keyword are:

*ISO: Date fields and literals are in International Standards Organization format (YYYY-MM-DD).

*MDY: Date fields and literals are in Month/Day/Year format (MM/DD/YY).

*DMY: Date fields and literals are in Day/Month/Year format (DD/MM/YY).

*YMD: Date fields and literals are in Year/Month/Day format (YY/MM/DD).

*JUL: Date fields and literals are in Julian format (YY/DDD).

*USA: Date fields and literals are in IBM USA Standard format (MM/DD/YYYY).

*EUR: Date fields and literals are in IBM European Standard format (DD.MM.YYYY).

*JIS: Date fields and literals are in Japanese Industrial Standard Christian Era format (YYYY-MM-DD).

The second parameter of the DATFMT keyword can be any single character. The default separator character depends on the date format specified. An ampersand separator character appears as a blank separator.

The H-spec in Figure 4.7 overrides the format of date literals and date fields in the program from *ISO to *JUL, and overrides the default separator character from a hyphen to a comma.

Figure 4.7: DATFMT Keyword Example

```
*. 1 ...+... 2 ...+... 3 ...+... 4 ...+... 5 ...+... 6 ...+... 7 ...+... 8
H DATFMT(*JUL,)
```

DEBUG (Debug)

Specifies whether or not DUMP operations are performed in the program. If the DEBUG keyword is not specified, or is specified with the *NO parameter, then DUMP operations are not performed. If the DEBUG keyword is specified without any parameters, or is specified with the *YES parameter, then DUMP operations are performed.

The possible DEBUG keyword parameter values are:

<u>***YES:**</u>   Use the DUMP operation.

*NO: Do not use the DUMP operation.

The H-spec in Figure 4.8 specifies that DUMP operations are performed in the program.

Figure 4.8: DEBUG Keyword Example

```
*. 1 ...+... 2 ...+... 3 ...+... 4 ...+... 5 ...+... 6 ...+... 7 ...+... 8
H DEBUG(*YES)
```

DECEDIT (Decimal Edit)

Specifies the character used for the decimal point in edited numbers and whether or not leading zeros are printed. If the DECEDIT keyword is not specified, then the period is used as a decimal point and leading zeros are not printed. If the DECEDIT keyword is specified, then it must be followed by a decimal point character in single quotes.

The possible DECEDIT keyword parameter values are:

'.':	Decimal point is a period and leading zeros are not printed.
',':	Decimal point is a comma and leading zeros are not printed.
'0.':	Decimal point is a period and leading zeros are printed.
'0,':	Decimal point is a comma and leading zeros are printed.

The H-spec in Figure 4.9 overrides the period decimal point character to a comma.

Figure 4.9: DECEDIT Keyword Example

```
*. 1 ...+... 2 ...+... 3 ...+... 4 ...+... 5 ...+... 6 ...+... 7 ...+... 8
H DECEDIT(',')
```

DFTNAME (Default Program Name)

Specifies the default program name when PGM(*CTLSPEC) is specified on the Create Bound RPG Program (CRTBNDRPG) command or the default module name when MODULE(*CTLSPEC) is specified on the Create RPG Module (CRTRPGMOD) command. If the DFTNAME keyword is not specified, then the default program name is RPGPGM and the default module name is RPGMOD.

The H-spec in Figure 4.10 specifies that the program or module be named ILE0301R when *CTLSPEC is specified on the program or module create command.

Figure 4.10: DFTNAME Keyword Example

```
*. 1 ...+... 2 ...+... 3 ...+... 4 ...+... 5 ...+... 6 ...+... 7 ...+... 8
H DFTNAME(ILE0301R)
```

FORMSALIGN (Forms Alignment)

Specifies that the first page of output causes the system to issue an alignment message for the spool file. If the FORMSALIGN keyword is not specified, or is specified with the *NO parameter, then the first page of output does not cause the system to issue an alignment message. If the FORMSALIGN keyword is specified, or is specified with the *YES parameter, then the first page of output causes the system to issue an alignment message.

The possible FORMSALIGN keyword parameter values are:

*YES: Issue an alignment message.

*NO: Do not issue an alignment message.

The H-spec in Figure 4.11 causes the system to issue an alignment message for the first page of output.

Figure 4.11: FORMSALIGN Keyword Example

```
*. 1 ...+... 2 ...+... 3 ...+... 4 ...+... 5 ...+... 6 ...+... 7 ...+... 8
H FORMSALIGN(*YES)
```

FTRANS (File Translation)

Specifies whether or not file translation takes place. If the FTRANS keyword is not specified, or is specified with the *NONE parameter, then file translation does not take place. If FTRANS(*SRC) is specified, then a file conversion table must be specified in the program.

The possible FTRANS keyword parameter values are:

*NONE: No file translation is requested.

*SRC: File translation is set to occur.

The H-spec in Figure 4.12 specifies that file translation is set to take place.

Figure 4.12: FTRANS Keyword Example

```
*. 1 ...+... 2 ...+... 3 ...+... 4 ...+... 5 ...+... 6 ...+... 7 ...+... 8
H FTRANS(*SRC)
```

TIMFMT (Time Format)

Specifies the format of time literals and time fields within the program. The default is *ISO format.

This keyword accepts two parameters. The first one is required, the second is optional. The first parameter specifies the time format, and the second parameter specifies the separator character. If the TIMFMT keyword is not specified, then the default time format is *ISO and the default separator character is a period. If the DATFMT keyword is specified, then it must be followed by a date format.

The possible values for the first parameter of the TIMFMT keyword are:

<u>*ISO:</u>	Time fields and literals are in International Standards Organization format (HH.MM.SS).
*HMS:	Time fields and literals are in Hour:Minute:Second format (HH:MM:SS).
*USA:	Time fields and literals are in IBM USA Standard format (HH:MM AM or HH:MM PM).
*EUR:	Time fields and literals are in IBM European Standard format (HH.MM.SS).
*JIS:	Time fields and literals are in Japanese Industrial Standard Christian Era format (HH:MM:SS).

The second parameter of the TIMFMT keyword can be any single character. The default separator character is a period.

The H-spec in Figure 4.13 overrides the default time format from *ISO to *USA.

Figure 4.13: TIMFMT Keyword Example

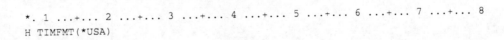

```
*. 1 ...+... 2 ...+... 3 ...+... 4 ...+... 5 ...+... 6 ...+... 7 ...+... 8
H TIMFMT(*USA)
```

SUMMARY

You have the choice of whether or not to code the H-spec, code a default H-spec in a source member or data area, or let the system use the default values for the H-spec keywords. H-specs now use keyword notation instead of the traditional fixed-format positional values. The H-spec can now span multiple lines of code. These changes simplify the coding of H-specs and make it easier for IBM to make enhancements to H-specs in the future.

Chapter 5

File Specification (F-spec)

The File specification (F-spec) describes the files used in the program. F-specs use a combination of fixed notation and keyword notation. The fixed notation portion extends from positions 7 through 42. Keywords are entered in positions 44 through 80. Figure 5.1 shows the general format of an ILE RPG file specification.

Figure 5.1: General F-spec Format

```
*. 1 ...+... 2 ...+... 3 ...+... 4 ...+... 5 ...+... 6 ...+... 7 ...+... 8
FFilename++IPEASFRlen+LKlen+AIDevice+.Keywords+++++++++++++++++++++++++++++
```

If you need more room for additional keywords, you can specify another F-spec using the format shown in Figure 5.2. To continue an F-spec line, leave positions 7 through 42 blank and specify additional keywords in positions 44 through 80.

Figure 5.2: F-spec Continuation Format

```
*. 1 ...+... 2 ...+... 3 ...+... 4 ...+... 5 ...+... 6 ...+... 7 ...+... 8
F.......................................Keywords+++++++++++++++++++++++++++++
```

EXAMPLE F-SPECS

The F-spec examples in Figures 5.3 and 5.4 show some of the differences between RPG/400 F-specs and ILE RPG F-specs. In the ILE RPG example, you can see further use of keyword notation.

Figure 5.3: RPG/400 F-specs

```
*. 1 ...+... 2 ...+... 3 ...+... 4 ...+... 5 ...+... 6 ...+... 7
FITEM01PFUF  E           K        DISK         KINFDS DSINFO
F                                              KINFSR ERRSUB
F            ITEMREC                           KRENAMEITEM1
```

Figure 5.4: ILE RPG F-specs

```
*. 1 ...+... 2 ...+... 3 ...+... 4 ...+... 5 ...+... 6 ...+... 7 ...+... 8
FITEM01PF  IF   E        K DISK   INFDS(DSINFO) INFSR(ERRSUB)
F                                 RENAME(ITEMREC:ITEM1)
```

The file information data structure DSINFO is now defined as a parameter of the INFDS keyword INFDS(DSINFO). In a similar manner, the information subroutine ERRSUB is now specified as a parameter on the INFSR keyword INFSR(ERRSUB). The rename of a record format is a two-part parameter of the RENAME keyword RENAME(ITEMREC:ITEM1).

The F-specs in ILE RPG have been modified to accommodate expanded lengths. For example, the eight-character file name in positions 7 through 14 has been expanded to 10 characters in positions 7 through 16. The four-character record length in positions 24 through 27 has been expanded to five characters in positions 23 through 27. And the two-character key length in positions 29 and 30 has been expanded to five characters in positions 29 through 33. There are other changes of this type, and other differences between RPG/400 and ILE RPG. Table 5.1 outlines these differences.

Table 5.1: Differences Between RPG/400 and ILE RPG F-specs

RPG/400 Positions	Description	ILE RPG Positions or Keyword
7 through 14	File name	7 through 16
15	File type	17
16	File designation	18
17	End of file control	19
18	Match field sequence	21
19	File format	22
24 through 27	Record length	23 through 27
28	Limits processing	28
29 and 30	Key field length	29 through 33
31	Record address type	34
32	File organization	35
33 and 34	Overflow indicator	OFLIND
35 through 38	Key field starting location	KEYLOC
39	Extension code	TOFILE FORMLEN FORMOFL
40 through 46	Device type	36 through 42
53 through 65	File continuation keywords	44 through 80
66	File additions	20
71 and 72	File condition	EXTIND
75 through 80	Comments	81 through 100

Figures 5.5 and 5.6 show the difference between RPG/400 and ILE RPG when a user-controlled file is specified.

Figure 5.5: RPG/400 F-specs

```
*. 1 ...+... 2 ...+... 3 ...+... 4 ...+... 5 ...+... 6 ...+... 7 .
FITEM01PFIF  E          K         DISK                          UC
FITEM02PFUF  E          K         DISK                      A   U1
```

Figure 5.6: ILE RPG F-specs

```
*. 1 ...+... 2 ...+... 3 ...+... 4 ...+... 5 ...+... 6 ...+... 7 ...+... 8
FITEM01PF  IF   E          K DISK    USROPN
FITEM02PF  UF A E          K DISK    EXTIND(*INU1)
```

The USROPN and EXTIND keywords are now used to condition the opening of files. The UC in positions 71 and 72 has been changed to the USROPN keyword for the file ITEM01PF. The U1 external indicator for file ITEM02PF has been changed to EXTIND(*INU1). This example also shows that, in order to specify that a file allow additions, an A is placed in position 20 rather than position 66.

FILE DESCRIPTION SPECIFICATION KEYWORDS

Many F-spec functions are expressed in keyword notation in ILE RPG. These keywords are shown in Table 5.2.

Table 5.2: F-spec Keywords

ILE RPG Keyword	Description
COMMIT	Commitment control
DATFMT	Date format
DEVID	Device id
EXTIND	External indicator
FORMLEN	Form length

ILE RPG Keyword	Description
FORMOFL	Form overflow line
IGNORE	Ignore record format
INCLUDE	Include record format
INFDS	File information data structure
INFSR	File exception/error subroutine
KEYLOC	Key location
MAXDEV	Maximum number of devices
OFLIND	Overflow indicator
PASS	Pass no indicators
PGMNAME	Program name
PLIST	Parameter list
PREFIX	Prefix
PRTCTL	Dynamic printer control
RAFDATA	Record address file data
RECNO	Record number
RENAME	Rename record format
SAVEDS	Save data structure
SAVEIND	Save indicators
SFILE	Subfile
SLN	Start line number
TIMFMT	Time format
USROPN	User-opened file

The following section describes most of the important file specification keywords with their associated parameters, and shows an example of how each keyword is used.

COMMIT (Commitment Control)

The COMIT keyword in RPG/400 has been changed to COMMIT in ILE RPG. Commitment control processing has been enhanced substantially through the ability to specify a single-character field as a parameter on the COMMIT keyword. The parameter sets a condition on the use of commitment control. If the field contains the value '1', the file is opened with commitment control. Otherwise, the file is opened without commitment control. The field value must be set prior to opening the file and can be passed as an *ENTRY parameter. If the file is shared and is already open, this keyword has no effect.

The F-spec in Figure 5.7 specifies that the file ITEM01PF may be opened under commitment control. If the value for the field ITMCMT is '1', either passed as an *ENTRY parameter or initialized on the D-spec, then the file is opened under commitment control. Otherwise, the file ITEM01PF is not opened under commitment control. If the file is opened explicitly, using the OPEN operation in the Calculation specifications, it can be set prior to the OPEN operation.

Figure 5.7: COMMIT Keyword Example

```
*. 1 ...+... 2 ...+... 3 ...+... 4 ...+... 5 ...+... 6 ...+... 7 ...+... 8
FITEM01PF  IF   E          K DISK    COMMIT(ITMCMT)
```

DATFMT (Date Format)

DATFMT allows the specification of a default date format and a default separator (which is optional). If the file on which this keyword is specified is indexed, and the key field is a date, then this also provides the default format for the key field. For program-described files, specify a D in position 34 for the record address type. If the DATFMT keyword is not specified, then the default date format is *ISO with a default date separator character of a hyphen.

The possible values for the first parameter of the DATFMT keyword are:

*ISO: Date fields and literals are in International Standards Organization format (YYYY-MM-DD).

*MDY: Date fields and literals are in Month/Day/Year format (MM/DD/YY).

*DMY: Date fields and literals are in Day/Month/Year format (DD/MM/YY).

*YMD: Date fields and literals are in Year/Month/Day format (YY/MM/DD).

*JUL: Date fields and literals are in Julian format (YY/DDD).

*USA: Date fields and literals are in IBM USA Standard format (MM/DD/YYYY).

*EUR: Date fields and literals are in IBM European Standard format (DD.MM.YYYY).

*JIS: Date fields and literals are in Japanese Industrial Standard Christian Era format (YYYY-MM-DD).

The second parameter of the DATFMT keyword can be any single character. The default separator character is a hyphen. An ampersand separator character appears as a blank separator.

The F-spec in Figure 5.8 specifies that the file EMPFILE is an indexed file with a date data type key field, which starts in position 41 for a length of eight. The F-spec also specifies that the default format for all date input fields is Year/Month/Day.

Figure 5.8: DATFMT Keyword Example

```
*. 1 ...+... 2 ...+... 3 ...+... 4 ...+... 5 ...+... 6 ...+... 7 ...+.. 8
FEMPFILE   IF   F   60      8DIDISK    KEYLOC(41) DATFMT(*YMD)
```

EXTIND (External Indicator)

The EXTIND keyword specifies whether or not the file should be opened at program initialization time. This keyword has a single parameter that must be specified. The possible parameter values are *INU1 through *INU8. If the value of the external indicator is on (1), then the file is automatically opened at program initialization. If the value is off (0), then the file is not opened. Use the SWS parameter of the Change Job (CHGJOB) command prior to calling the program to set the values of indicators U1 through U8. For example, to set on indicator U1 prior to calling an ILE RPG program, run the following command:

```
CHGJOB SWS(1XXXXXXX)
```

The example in Figure 5.9 uses the EXTIND keyword to specify that the file ITEM01PF is only opened when the value of *INU1 is equal to 1.

Figure 5.9: EXTIND Keyword Example

```
 *. 1 ...+... 2 ...+... 3 ...+... 4 ...+... 5 ...+... 6 ...+... 7 ...+.. 8
FITEM01PF  IF   E          K DISK    EXTIND(*INU1)
```

FORMLEN (Form Length)

The L-spec has been eliminated from ILE RPG and its function has been moved to the F-spec. The FORMLEN keyword specifies the form length of a printer file. The valid values are between 1 and 255. In Figure 5.10, the form length is set to 66 lines.

Figure 5.10: FORMLEN Keyword Example

```
 *. 1 ...+... 2 ...+... 3 ...+... 4 ...+... 5 ...+... 6 ...+... 7 ...+.. 8
FQPRINT   O   F 132        PRINTER FORMLEN(66)
```

FORMOFL (Form Overflow)

The FORMOFL keyword sets the overflow line number of a printer file. The values must be less than or equal to the value of the form length. In Figure 5.11, the form length is set to 66 lines and the overflow line number is set to 60.

Figure 5.11: FORMOFL Keyword Example

```
*. 1 ...+... 2 ...+... 3 ...+... 4 ...+... 5 ...+... 6 ...+... 7 ...+.. 8
FQPRINT    O  F 132       PRINTER FORMLEN(66) FORMOFL(60)
```

IGNORE (Ignore Record Format)

This keyword allows you to ignore one or more record formats in a file. When a record format name is specified for the IGNORE keyword, the compiler does not bring in the external definition of that format. You can not use the INCLUDE keyword with the IGNORE keyword; they are mutually exclusive.

In Figure 5.12, the record format ITEMREC for file ITEM02LF is ignored. To ignore more than one record format, separate the record format names with a colon (:). For example, IGNORE (ITEMREC1:ITEMREC2) ignores two record formats.

Figure 5.12: IGNORE Keyword Example

```
*. 1 ...+... 2 ...+... 3 ...+... 4 ...+... 5 ...+... 6 ...+... 7 ...+.. 8
FITEM02LF IF   E       K DISK    IGNORE(ITEMREC)
```

INCLUDE (Include Record Format)

This keyword allows you to include one or more record formats in a file. All other record formats in the file that are not specified on this keyword are ignored. When a record format name is specified for the INCLUDE keyword, the compiler brings in the external definition of that format. You can not use the IGNORE keyword with the INCLUDE keyword; they are mutually exclusive. In Figure 5.13, the record format ITEMREC for file ITEM02LF is included. All other record formats in ITEM02LF are ignored.

Figure 5.13: INCLUDE Keyword Example

```
*. 1 ...+... 2 ...+... 3 ...+... 4 ...+... 5 ...+... 6 ...+... 7 ...+.. 8
FITEM02LF IF   E       K DISK    INCLUDE(ITEMREC)
```

INFDS (File Information Data Structure)

This keyword specifies the name of a data structure to contain file information. In Figure 5.14, the ITEM01PF file specifies the file information data structure FILEINFO for the INFDS keyword. The FILEINFO data structure contains a subfield called FILENAME. This subfield contains the name of the file from the file information data structure.

Figure 5.14: INFDS Keyword Example

```
*. 1 ...+... 2 ...+... 3 ...+... 4 ...+... 5 ...+... 6 ...+... 7 ...+.. 8
FITEM01PF  IF   E           K DISK    INFDS(FILEINFO)
DFILEINFO        DS
D  FILENAME        *FILE
```

INFSR (File Exception Subroutine)

This keyword specifies the name of a subroutine that receives control when a file exception error occurs. In Figure 5.15, the ITEM01PF file specifies the subroutine *PSSR, the default user-written exception subroutine, on the INFSR keyword. The program executes the *PSSR subroutine if an exception error occurs for file ITEM01PF.

Figure 5.15: INFSR Keyword Example

```
*. 1 ...+... 2 ...+... 3 ...+... 4 ...+... 5 ...+... 6 ...+... 7 ...+.. 8
FITEM01PF  IF   E           K DISK    INFSR(*PSSR)
 *                            .
 *                            .
 *                            .
C     *PSSR        BEGSR
C                  ENDSR
```

OFLIND (Overflow Indicator)

This keyword specifies the overflow indicator assigned to a printer file. The valid parameter values are *INOA through *INOG, *INOV, and *IN01 through *IN99. In Figure 5.16, the printer file QPRINT specifies the *IN90 indicator on the OFLIND keyword. RPG sets on *IN90 when QPRINT reaches the overflow line.

Figure 5.16: OFLIND Keyword Example

```
*. 1 ...+... 2 ...+... 3 ...+... 4 ...+... 5 ...+... 6 ...+... 7 ...+.. 8
FQPRINT    O   F 132      PRINTER OFLIND(*IN90)
```

PREFIX (Prefix)

This keyword allows you to rename the fields in an externally described file. The value you specify as the parameter is used as a prefix to all of the fields in the file. An exception to this rule is that fields that are explicitly renamed in I-specs are not renamed by the PREFIX keyword. Be aware that, with the PREFIX keyword, the length of the prefix plus the length of the externally described field can not exceed 10 characters.

Figure 5.17 shows two file specifications. The fields in the physical file ITEM01PF are renamed with a prefix of P_. The fields in the logical file ITEM02LF are renamed with a prefix of L_.

Figure 5.17: PREFIX Keyword Example

```
*. 1 ...+... 2 ...+... 3 ...+... 4 ...+... 5 ...+... 6 ...+... 7 ...+.. 8
FITEM01PF  IF   E      K DISK      PREFIX(P_)
FITEM02LF  IF   E      K DISK      PREFIX(L_) RENAME(ITEMREC:ITEM02)
```

Look at the partial compile listing in Figure 5.18. You can see the results of using the PREFIX keyword. The fields ITNUM, ITDESC, and ITAMT for file ITEM01PF are renamed to P_ITNUM, P_ITDESC, and P_ITAMT. In a similar manner, the fields ITNUM, ITDESC, and ITAMT for file ITEM02LF are renamed to L_ITNUM, L_ITDESC, and L_ITAMT.

Figure 5.18: Results of Using the PREFIX Keyword

```
*. 1 ...+... 2 ...+... 3 ...+... 4 ...+... 5 ...+... 6 ...+... 7 ...+.. 8
FITEM01PF  IF   E      K DISK      PREFIX(P_)
*------------------------------------------------------------
*                          RPG name         External name
* File name. . . . . . . . :  ITEM01PF       ILERPG/ITEM01PF
* Record format(s) . . . . :  ITEMREC        ITEMREC
*------------------------------------------------------------
FITEM02LF  IF   E      K DISK      PREFIX(L_) RENAME(ITEMREC:ITEM02)
*------------------------------------------------------------
```

```
*                         RPG name        External name
* File name. . . . . . . . . :  ITEM02LF        ILERPG/ITEM02LF
* Record format(s) . . . . . :  ITEM02          ITEMREC
*_____
IITEMREC
 *_____
* RPG record format  . . . . :  ITEMREC
* Prefix . . . . . . . . . . :  P_
* External format  . . . . . :  ITEMREC : ILERPG/ITEM01PF
 *_____
I                         P   1    2 0P_ITNUM
I                         A   3   42  P_ITDESC
I                         P  43   46 2P_ITAMT
IITEM02
 *_____
* RPG record format  . . . . :  ITEM02
* Prefix . . . . . . . . . . :  L_
* External format  . . . . . :  ITEMREC : ILERPG/ITEM02LF
 *_____
I                         P   1    2 0L_ITNUM
I                         A   3   42  L_ITDESC
I                         P  43   46 2L_ITAMT
C               EVAL      *INLR = *ON
* * * * *   E N D   O F   S O U R C E   * * * * *
```

RENAME (Rename Record Format)

The RENAME keyword allows you to change a record format name used in an externally described file. This keyword requires two parameters separated by a colon. The first parameter specifies the name of the external record format. The second parameter specifies the new name for the external record format. This keyword is useful when you have two files with the same record format name. This is often the case when you are using a physical file and a logical file in the same program where the logical file is based on the physical file. RPG does not allow two files to have the same format name, so you have to rename one of them. Figure 5.19 shows file specifications for ITEM01PF and ITEM02LF. In this case, ITEM02LF is based on ITEM01PF, and both files have the same record format name of ITEMREC. On the F-spec for ITEM02LF, you can see that the RENAME keyword is used to rename the ITEMREC format to ITEM02.

Figure 5.19: RENAME Keyword Example

```
*. 1 ...+... 2 ...+... 3 ...+... 4 ...+... 5 ...+... 6 ...+... 7 ...+.. 8
FITEM01PF  IF   E          K DISK
FITEM02LF  IF   E          K DISK    RENAME(ITEMREC:ITEM02)
```

SFILE (Subfile)

The SFILE keyword identifies any subfiles used in a display file that you want to use in an RPG program. This keyword requires two parameters separated by a colon. The first parameter specifies the name of the subfile record format. The second parameter specifies the name of a field used to store the relative record number of the subfile records. RPG loads this field on input operations such as READC or CHAIN. This field is also where you load the relative record number of when you issue an output operation to a subfile using the WRITE operation code. The subfile relative record number field must be defined in the program with zero decimal positions. It must also be defined large enough to hold the value of the highest subfile record used in the program. In Figure 5.20, file ILE0401D uses the SFILE keyword to identify the subfile record format ILESFL and the subfile relative record number field RRN.

Figure 5.20: SFILE Keyword Example

```
*. 1 ...+... 2 ...+... 3 ...+... 4 ...+... 5 ...+... 6 ...+... 7 ...+.. 8
FILE0401D  CF   E           WORKSTN SFILE(ILESFL:RRN)
```

TIMFMT (Time Format)

TIMFMT allows the specification of a default time format and a default separator (which is optional). If the file on which this keyword is specified is indexed, and the key field is a time, then this also provides the default format for the key field. For program-described files, specify a T in position 34 for the record address type. If the TIMFMT is not specified, then the default time format is *ISO with a default date separator of a period.

The possible values for the first parameter of the TIMFMT keyword are:

*ISO: Time fields and literals are in International Standards Organization format (HH.MM.SS).

*HMS: Time fields and literals are in Hour:Minute:Second format (HH:MM:SS).

*USA: Time fields and literals are in IBM USA Standard format (HH:MM AM or HH:MM PM).

*EUR: Time fields and literals are in IBM European Standard format (HH.MM.SS).

> ***JIS:**   Time fields and literals are in Japanese Industrial
>   Standard Christian Era format (HH:MM:SS).

Depending on the time format, the second parameter of the TIMFMT keyword can be a colon, period, or comma. An ampersand separator character appears as a blank separator.

The F-spec in Figure 5.21 specifies that the file EMPFILE is an indexed file with a time data type key field, which starts in position 41 for a length of eight. The F-spec also specifies that the default format for all time input fields is Hour:Minute:Second.

Figure 5.21: TIMFMT Keyword Example

```
*. 1 ...+... 2 ...+... 3 ...+... 4 ...+... 5 ...+... 6 ...+... 7 ...+.. 8
FEMPFILE   IF   F   60     8DIDISK    KEYLOC(41) TIMFMT(*HMS)
```

USROPN (User Open)

The USROPN keyword specifies that the file is not opened at program initialization time. When this keyword is used, the file must be opened using the OPEN operation. Figure 5.22 uses the USROPN keyword to specify that the file ITEM01PF is not opened at program initialization time.

Figure 5.22: USROPN Keyword Example

```
*. 1 ...+... 2 ...+... 3 ...+... 4 ...+... 5 ...+... 6 ...+... 7 ...+.. 8
FITEM01PF  IF   E          K DISK    USROPN
```

SUMMARY

As you can see, F-specs have undergone some significant changes. The use of keyword notation facilitates coding F-specs while making them more readable. Changes to accommodate longer file names eliminate the need to perform file overrides at compile time and run time. Additional functions, such as the ability to include record formats and prefix fields selectively, bring powerful new capabilities to F-specs.

Chapter 6

Definition Specification (D-spec)

The new Definition specification (D-spec) is used to consolidate all data definitions into one section of your program. (Even though you can still define variables in C-specs, the ability to group constant and variable declarations makes using D-specs a better coding practice.) With the D-spec, you can define stand-alone fields, data structures, data structure subfields, named constants, arrays, tables, and pointers. Having the ability to define all program-described variables with one specification type, and in the same section of a program, can help to make a program easier to read. D-specs replace E-specs, which have been eliminated, and take over some functions from RPG/400, I-specs, and C-specs. In addition, D-specs provide new ways to define some data constructs.

You no longer have to remember all of the different formats of the I-spec. Other than variables from externally described files, you can go to one section of an RPG/400 program and analyze your variable. (Externally described files still generate I-specs, which the compiler inserts after the D-spec.)

Using keywords, you can supplement the definition of a variable. For example, you can add formatting to a date or time variable with the DATFMT and TIMFMT keywords. You can turn a variable into an array using the DIM keyword.

Table 6.1 illustrates the general format of the D-spec and the absolute position of each entry.

Table 6.1: D-spec Format

Statement Positions	Purpose	Valid Entries
6	**Definition specification**	D
7 through 21	Name of field, array, table, named constant, data structure, or data structure subfield.	Any valid symbolic name
22	**Data structure identification** Externally described data structure. Program-described data structure.	 E Blank
23	**Type of data structure** Program status data structure. Data area data structure. Non-program status or data area data structure.	 S U Blank
24 through 25	**Type of definition** Stand-alone field or array. Named constant. Data structure. Data structure subfield.	 S C DS Blank
26 through 32	**From position/keyword** Variable length is defined by value specified in the To position, or the variable is defined elsewhere. Absolute starting position. Keywords for file information and program status data structure subfields.	Blank 1 through 9999999 *PROC, *STATUS, etc.

Statement Positions	Purpose	Valid Entries
33 through 39	**To position/length** Data structure specifications: field defined LIKE another field, field length implied, attributes of field defined elsewhere.	Blank
	Absolute end position if starting position is specified, length of field if From is blank, length specification for an entire data structure.	1 through 9999999
	Increase or decrease field size when defining a field LIKE another field.	+/- 1 through 99999
40	**Internal type of field, subfield, or array element** If the decimal position is blank, the type is character unless the LIKE keyword is used. If decimal position is non-blank, the field is a stand-alone field; the type is packed, or zoned if the field is a subfield of a data structure.	Blank
	Character Graphic character Time Date Time stamp Packed decimal Binary Zoned decimal Pointer	A G T D Z P B S *
41 and 42	**Decimal positions**	0 through 30
44 through 80	**Keywords**	Any valid D-spec keyword
81 through 100	**Comments**	Optional

In the following sections, we look at simple data constructs, such as named constants and work fields, then at more complex examples, such as data structures and arrays. Both an RPG/400 and an ILE RPG solution are shown whenever possible. However, the explanation of each example concentrates on the ILE RPG implementation.

Named Constants

In RPG/400, named constants can appear anywhere in I-specs, even within a data structure definition. In ILE RPG, named constants can not appear within a data structure definition. If the RPG/400-to-ILE RPG source-conversion utility finds named constants embedded in a data structure, it moves the named constants outside of the data structure as part of the source-conversion process.

Figure 6.1 shows how to define several named constants: the character constants CMPNY and LWR, the numeric constant TWENTY, and the hexadecimal constant DUP.

Figure 6.1: Definitions of Named Constants

RPG/400

```
*.. 1 ...+... 2 ...+... 3 ...+... 4 ...+... 5 ...+... 6 ...+... 7 ...+... 8
I..............Namedconstant++++++++C.........Fldnme....................
I              'Midrange Computing'  C         CMPNY
I              'abcdefghijklmnopqrs- C         LWR
I              'tuvwxyz'
I              20                    C         TWENTY
I              X'1C'                 C         DUP
```

ILE RPG

```
*.. 1 ...+... 2 ...+... 3 ...+... 4 ...+... 5 ...+... 6 ...+... 7 ...+... 8
DName+++++++++++ETDsFrom+++To/L+++IDc.Keywords++++++++++++++++++++++++++++++
D CMPNY           C               CONST('Midrange Computing')
D LWR             C               'abcdefghijklmnopqrs-
D                                 tuvwxyz'
D
D TWENTY          C               CONST(20)
D DUP             C               X'1C'
```

Only a few entries are required:

♦   The C in position 24 defines a named constant.

♦   The value entered for the CONST keyword defines the value of the constant. Although a value is required for the constant, you do not have to preface the value with the CONST keyword.

The CONST keyword defines a character string for the first constant, CMPNY. The second example of a constant, LWR, includes several variations.

- The CONST keyword is omitted and the character constant is defined by enclosing the literal value in single quotes.

- The trailing hyphen indicates that the value continues on the next line, starting with the first character of the functions section (position 44). (Note that the constant on the continuation line *does not* start with a quote as it does in RPG/400.)

The final two examples show the definition of noncharacter constants. The numeric constant TWENTY is defined by specifying a numeric value not enclosed in single quotes. Hexadecimal constants can be defined by specifying an X followed by a valid hexadecimal value enclosed in single quotes. In the example, DUP is defined as a hexadecimal constant with a value of X'1C' to represent the character returned when the DUP key is pressed. The actual CONST keyword is optional for all constants, regardless of data type.

STAND-ALONE FIELDS

Traditionally, RPG programmers have defined work fields in C-specs. Although this is still possible using ILE RPG, you can define stand-alone fields that are not part of any file or data structure in D-specs. Figure 6.2 provides several examples.

Figure 6.2: Defining Stand-alone Fields

RPG/400

```
IDsname....NODsExt-file++.............OccrLen+.......
I           DS
I ............Ext-field+.....................Field+
I                           P   1   42PACK72
CL0N01N02N03Factor1+++OpcdeFactor2+++ResultLenDHHiLoEq
C           *LIKE     DEFN PRGROS     LRGROS+ 2
C           *LIKE     DEFN PRNAME     XXNAME
C                     MOVEL'Missing' XXNAME      P
```

ILE RPG

```
DName+++++++++++ETDsFrom+++To/L+++IDc.Keywords++++++++++++++++++++++++++++++
D PACK72         S              7P 2
D LRGROS         S              +2      LIKE(PRGROS)
D XXNAME         S                      LIKE(PRNAME) INZ('Missing')
```

One special entry is required to define a stand-alone field—an S in position 24. The first example in Figure 6.2 is a seven-digit work field (PACK72). Field PACK72 is stored in packed-decimal format and has two decimal places. In RPG/400 you are forced to define this field in C-specs or make this field part of a data structure even though it does not logically need to be associated with any other field.

The length of the field is coded in positions 33 to 39, rather than using starting and ending positions. The positions within the D-specs are different than those for I-specs, but contain the same type of entries.

The second example defines LRGROS based on the field PRGROS. LRGROS is defined as two character positions greater than PRGROS. ILE RPG permits you to use either the LIKE keyword in D-specs or the *LIKE DEFINE operation in C-specs to define a field based on the characteristics of another field.

The final example of a stand-alone field, illustrated in Figure 6.2, defines XXNAME with the same characteristics as the field PRNAME. One new keyword, INZ, is added for this example. This keyword specifies the value to which a field is initialized. Initializing fields using this method is more efficient than initializing them in the C-specs. When the INZ keyword is not specified, the default value is blank for character fields and 0 for numeric fields.

ORGANIZING DATA

Complex data organizations are one of the primary reasons for adding D-specs to the RPG language definition.

Data Structures

The first of these data organizations that we examine is the data structure. Figure 6.3 illustrates two ways to code a data structure in ILE RPG.

Figure 6.3: Coding Data Structures

RPG/400

```
*.. 1 ...+... 2 ...+... 3 ...+... 4 ...+... 5 ...+... 6 ...+... 7 ...+... 8
IDsname....NODsExt-file++.............OccrLen+.......
IGLDS        DS
I..............Ext-field+....................Field+
I                              1  30 GLDESC
I                             31  41 GLNUM
I                             31  32 GLCMPY
I                             33  36 GLMAIN
I                             37  41 GLSUB
I                             42  44 GLCLAS
I                             45  48 GLCAT
```

ILE RPG

```
DName+++++++++++ETDsFrom+++To/L+++IDc.Keywords++++++++++++++++++++++++
 *
 * Sample using absolute notation
 *
D glds            DS
D   gldesc                 1      30
D   glnum                 31      41
D     glcmpy              31      32
D     glmain              33      36
D     glsub               37      41
D   glclas                42      44
D   glcat                 45      48
 *
 * Sample using length notation
 *
D glds            DS
D   gldesc                        30
D   glnum                         11
D     glcmpy                       2  OVERLAY(GLNUM)
D     glmain                       4  OVERLAY(GLNUM:3)
D     glsub                        5  OVERLAY(GLNUM:7)
D   glclas                         3
D   glcat                          4
```

In the first example, the ILE RPG code is very similar to the RPG/400 code. Absolute From and To positions are used to designate the starting and ending positions of each subfield. The differences between the RPG/400 example and the ILE RPG example are based on general rules for formatting ILE RPG.

♦ Subfields may be indented to make the data structure easier to understand.

♦ Lowercase or uppercase field names may be used. The compiler translates lowercase field names to uppercase.

The second ILE RPG example takes advantage of two new features. Length notation is used instead of specifying the starting and ending positions for each field. The length of each subfield is specified in positions 33 through 39. The rest of the syntax is identical to absolute notation (for example, coding a P for packed data, specifying decimal positions).

The OVERLAY keyword further subdivides a subfield within a data structure. The first parameter indicates the name of the subfield whose storage is to be overlaid. This subfield must have been defined previously in the same data structure. For example, in Figure 6.3, GLNUM was defined prior to its use in the OVERLAY keyword for field glcmpy. The second parameter specifies the starting position within the field. The starting position is optional and the default is 1.

In this example, OVERLAY(GLNUM) is specified for the field glcmpy. Because glcmpy has a length of two and the starting position defaults to 1, the field glcmpy is defined as the first two positions of the field glnum. For the field glmain, OVERLAY(GLNUM:3) is specified. Because glmain has a length of four and the starting position is 3, the field glmain is defined as positions 3 through 6 of the field glnum. Finally, the field glsub is defined as positions 7 through 11 of the field glnum.

When using the OVERLAY keyword, the subfield being defined may not extend beyond the end of the field being overlaid. In the example, specifying OVERLAY(GLNUM:8) for the field glsub causes an error. Because glsub is a five-character field, starting in position 8 extends this field to position 12. An error occurs because glnum is only 11 characters long.

When length notation is used, changes to the starting position within the field glnum do not affect subsequent fields that are not part of glnum. Overlaid fields, however, are affected. For example, if you increase the length of glnum to 13 and of glmain to 6, you may need to change the starting position of glsub so that glmain and glsub do not overlap. No changes are required for the fields glclas and glcat.

Length notation makes future modifications easier than if absolute notation is used. When the length of a field changes, subsequent fields do not have to be modified. In this example, the field gldesc could be expanded to 40 positions without making any changes to the definition of glnum or its subfields.

Figure 6.4 illustrates an externally defined data structure. The ILE RPG portion of this example uses several keywords described in previous examples. One new keyword is introduced.

Figure 6.4: Externally Defined Data Structures

External Data Structure DDS for OELPMNM

```
...1 ...+... 2 ...+... 3 ...+... 4 ...+... 5 ...+... 6 ...+... 7 ...+... 8
A          R PMT
A            PMTNUM        3 0
A            PMTZIP        9
```

RPG/400

```
...1 ...+... 2 ...+... 3 ...+... 4 ...+... 5 ...+... 6 ...+... 7 ...+... 8
IDsname....NODsExt-file++.............OccrLen+...........................
I          EIDSOELPMNM
I..............Ext-field+...........PFromTo++DField+....................
I            PMTNUM                         P2TNUM
I            PMTZIP                         P2TZIP
```

ILE RPG

Source Definition of External Data Structure

```
DName++++++++++ETDsFrom+++To/L+++IDc.Keywords++++++++++++++++++++++++

D            E DS                   EXTNAME(OELPMNM) PREFIX(P2_)
```

Partial Compile Listing

```
D            E DS                   EXTNAME(OELPMNM) PREFIX(P2_)
*_____
* Data structure . . . . . . :
* Prefix . . . . . . . . . . : P2_
* External format . . . . . : PMT : ILERPG/OELPMNM
*_____
D P2_PMTNUM                 3P 0
D P2_PMTZIP                 9A
```

By analyzing the partial compile listing, you can see how the externally defined data structure is imported by the compiler.

♦ The E in position 22 specifies that this is an externally defined data structure.

◆ The EXTNAME keyword indicates that the data structure is defined
    based on the definition of the first (or only) record format of the file
    OELPMNM. To define explicitly the record used, you might code
    EXTNAME (OELPMNM:OELPMNM9), indicating that record format
    OELPMNM9 is used even if it is not the first record format in the file.

◆ The PREFIX keyword implicitly renames the fields in the data structure.
    This global rename function is similar to the PREFIX keyword used in
    F-specs (see Chapter 5). PMTNUM is renamed P2_PMTNUM,
    PMTZIP is renamed P2_PMTZIP, and PMTZIP is renamed
    P2_PMTZIP.

The example in Figure 6.5 associates a data structure with an external data area. One
new keyword is used.

Figure 6.5: Describing Data Areas

RPG/400

```
... 1 ...+... 2 ...+... 3 ...+... 4 ...+... 5 ...+... 6 ...+... 7 ...+... 8
IDsname....NODsExt-file++..............OccrLen+...........................
IINV#DS     UDS
I...........Ext-field+..............PFromTo++DField+L1M1..PlMnZr..........
I                             1   70$INV#
I                             8   8 $ISTS

CL0N01N02N03Factor1+++OpcdeFactor2+++ResultLenDEHiLoEqComments++++++++......
C           *NAMVAR   DEFN OEAIN    INV#DS           Invoice # DTAARA
```

ILE RPG

```
DName++++++++++ETDsFrom+++To/L+++IDc.Keywords++++++++++++++++++++++++++

D INV#DS          UDS                  DTAARA(OEAIN)
D   $INV#                       7S 0
D   $ISTS                       1A
```

As you can see, the ILE RPG definition of a data area is more intuitive; and, there's
no need for a C-spec to link the data area to the data structure.

◆ The U in position 23 indicates the data structure is a data area.

◆ The DTAARA keyword can be used to specify the name of a data area.
    Special parameter values for this keyword are *LDA for the local data
    area and *PDA for the PIP (program initialization parameters) data area.

ILE RPG permits you to use either the DTAARA keyword in D-specs or the *DTAARA DEFINE operation in C-specs to associate external data areas with internal program structures.

Arrays and Tables

In this section, we look at several examples of data organization by arrays and tables, and the new capabilities that ILE RPG provides for them. The essential definition of arrays has not changed. ILE RPG supports the three types of arrays (compile-time, prerun-time, and run-time) currently available with RPG/400. The same basic rules apply. However, ILE RPG uses keywords to define the number of elements, From and To files, and the type of array. As in RPG/400, a table is defined when its name begins with the letters TAB. We refer to tables and arrays generically as arrays unless an example specifically uses a table.

Figure 6.6 shows a run-time array coded in RPG/400 using an E-spec, and coded in ILE RPG using a D-spec. This example illustrates the new structure of array definitions.

Figure 6.6: Run-time Array

RPG/400

```
... 1 ...+... 2 ...+... 3 ...+... 4 ...+... 5 ...+... 6 ...+... 7 ...+... 8
E....FromfileTofile++Name++N/rN/tbLenPDSArrnamLenPDSComments+++++++++......
E                   DEPT      10 2
```

ILE RPG

```
DName+++++++++++ETDsFrom+++To/L+++IDc.Keywords++++++++++++++++++++++++
DDEPT             S             2    DIM(10)
```

The D-spec is used to define an array along with any other program variables that might be defined. There is no need to use a different specification (E-spec) as was required in RPG/400.

♦ The S in position 24 of the D-spec has the same meaning as it has for stand-alone fields. It indicates that the array is not part of a data structure.

♦ The length for each element is coded in positions 33 through 39.

♦ The DIM keyword defines the dimension (the number of elements) of the array.

Figure 6.7 shows a compile-time array. Several new keywords are required to define how the compile-time array data is included in the source code.

♦ The CTDATA keyword indicates that the array is loaded from compile-time data included at the end of the source member.

♦ The PERRCD keyword is used for compile-time and prerun-time arrays to specify the number of elements loaded from each record. The default is PERRCD(1) when CTDATA is specified, so this parameter does not have to be coded. It is included here to make the code easier to understand.

♦ The ASCEND keyword signifies that the array is in ascending sequence. Using the DESCEND keyword designates descending sequence.

Figure 6.7: Compile-time Array

RPG/400

```
... 1 ...+... 2 ...+... 3 ...+... 4 ...+... 5 ...+... 6 ...+... 7 ...+... 8
E....FromfileTofile++Name++N/rN/tbLenPDSArrnamLenPDSComments+++++++++......
E                   DEPT    1 10 2 A
```

ILE RPG

```
DName+++++++++++ETDsFrom+++To/L+++IDc.Keywords+++++++++++++++++++++++++
DDEPT             S            2    DIM(10) CTDATA PERRCD(1) ASCEND
```

Figure 6.8 introduces additional information on how to define prerun-time arrays and how to initialize run-time arrays.

Figure 6.8: Prerun-time Arrays

RPG/400

```
... 1 ...+... 2 ...+... 3 ...+... 4 ...+... 5 ...+... 6 ...+... 7 ...+... 8
E....FromfileTofile++Name++N/rN/tbLenPDSArrnamLenPDSComments+++++++++......
E    OLDDEPT       TABDPT 1 100  3 0ATABTOT  9P2
```

ILE RPG

```
DName++++++++++ETDsFrom+++To/L+++IDc.Keywords+++++++++++++++++++++++++++
D TABDPT          S              3 0 DIM(100) PERRCD (1) ASCEND FROMFILE
D                                     (OLDDEPT)
D TABTOT          S              9 2 DIM(100) ALT(TABDPT) EXTFMT(P)
```

This example loads two tables (everything in this example is valid for arrays as well as tables) from a file at prerun-time. The data is loaded the first time the program is called. There are three new keywords:

♦   The ALT keyword is specified to associate the alternating table TABTOT with the primary table TABDPT.

♦   FROMFILE(OLDDEPT) causes the tables TABDPT and TABTOT to load from the file OLDDEPT when the program is called for the first time.

♦   The EXTFMT keyword can be used to specify the external data format for compile-time and prerun-time arrays. In this example, EXTFMT(P) specified for the table TABTOT indicates that data elements of this table are stored in packed, decimal format in the file OLDDEPT. Other formats, including the new date and time-stamp formats, are also valid.

In this example, PERRCD (1) specifies that one element of each table is loaded from each record of the file OLDDEPT.

The keywords for the table TABDPT continue on a second line. If positions 7 through 43 of a D-spec are blank, the compiler interprets the line as a continuation of the previous line. In fact, a keyword can be coded on one line with its parameter coded on the next line, as in the case of the keyword FROMFILE and its parameter OLDDEPT. However, coding in this manner is not recommended as it can be confusing; the code is included here for illustration only. ILE RPG also permits spaces between the keyword and its parameter, as shown with the PERRCD keyword.

Figure 6.9 shows the run-time array SRT. Because this is a run-time array, the PERRCD keyword is not allowed.

There is one new keyword in this example. The INZ keyword permits different initialization values to be specified for the array. In the ILE RPG example, the *HIVAL default value is specified for compile time, instead of using MOVE in the C-specs at run time, as shown in the RPG/400 example.

Figure 6.9: Initializing a Run-time Array

RPG/400

```
... 1 ...+... 2 ...+... 3 ...+... 4 ...+... 5 ...+... 6 ...+... 7 ...+... 8
E....FromfileTofile++Name++N/rN/tbLenPDSArrnamLenPDSComments++++++++......
E                       SRT       99 10
CL0N01N02N03Factor1+++OpcdeFactor2+++ResultLenDEHiLoEqComments++++++......
C           *INZSR    BEGSR
C                     MOVE *HIVAL    SRT
C                     ENDSR
```

ILE RPG

```
DName+++++++++++ETDsFrom+++To/L+++IDc.Keywords++++++++++++++++++++++++++
D SRT             S             10A   DIM(99) INZ(*HIVAL)
```

The INZ keyword causes initialization of the array with the specified value the first time the program is called. If the program returns without setting on the indicator LR and is called again, the INZ keyword has no effect the second time the program is called. The array has the same value it had when the program last returned. By default, the initialization values are based on the data type—blanks for character data and zeros for numeric data. To illustrate this point, the example defines SRT explicitly as a character array with the data type of A in position 40. The data type is optional because, as in DDS, a field with no decimal positions specified defaults to a character field.

IMPORTS AND EXPORTS

Imports and exports can be used to pass fields or data structures between one ILE RPG module and another. The use of imports and exports is similar in concept to parameter passing. One module defines the storage for a data item and exports it to another module. The second module then imports the data item and can access the same storage variable.

There must be a one-to-one relationship between imports and exports. If a field is defined as an import but no module in the program contains an export definition of the same name, an error occurs at compile time.

The IMPORT keyword specifies that storage for the data item being defined is allocated in another module, but may be accessed in this module. The EXPORT keyword allows a data item defined within a module to be used by another module in the program. The storage for the data item is allocated in the module containing the EXPORT definition.

Let's look at an example to see how the IMPORT and EXPORT keywords can be used. Figure 6.10 shows an example of a module that uses the EXPORT keyword to export a field called COUNT. This module drops into a loop that repeats until the COUNT field reaches 1,000. Within the loop, the CALLB operation is used to call a second module (MOD2) shown in Figure 6.11. In MOD2, the IMPORT keyword is used to import the COUNT field. This module increments the COUNT field by a value of 1 and passes control back to the first module. After the CALLB to MOD2 in the first module, the value of COUNT is one greater than before the CALLB instruction. When COUNT reaches 1,000, the program ends.

Figure 6.10: EXPORT Keyword Example

```
*. 1 ...+... 2 ...+... 3 ...+... 4 ...+... 5 ...+... 6 ...+... 7
D COUNT           S              7P 0 EXPORT

C                 DOU           COUNT = 1000
C                 CALLB         'MOD2'
C                 ENDDO

C                 EVAL          *INLR = *ON
```

Figure 6.11: IMPORT Keyword Example

```
*. 1 ...+... 2 ...+... 3 ...+... 4 ...+... 5 ...+... 6 ...+... 7
D COUNT           S              7P 0 IMPORT

C                 EVAL          COUNT = COUNT + 1

C                 EVAL          *INLR = *ON
```

This example shows you how the IMPORT and EXPORT keywords can be used to share data between modules. The same results could have been obtained by passing a parameter on the CALLB instruction and adding an *ENTRY parameter to MOD2. However, through the use of the binder language (see Chapter 2) you have greater control over which variables are available to other modules, thereby providing greater flexibility than passing parameters.

SUMMARY

The new D-specs permit you to consolidate data definitions in your programs, which can make them easier to understand and modify. In addition, the OVERLAY, PREFIX, and length notations provide substantial usability improvements in ILE RPG.

Chapter 7

Input Specification (I-spec)

This chapter looks at the ILE RPG Input specification (I-spec). For the ILE RPG programmer, the I-spec plays a much less important role than it did in previous versions of RPG. Originally, the I-spec was used to define record and field information. As time went on, other uses for the I-spec were created, including defining data structures, data areas, and named constants. In fact, the I-spec in RPG/400 ended up serving too many purposes. The last time we counted, there were eight different I-spec formats from which to choose. Fortunately, as you learned in the last chapter, the D-spec consolidates the numerous I-spec formats into one data definition specification that is much easier to understand. You still see I-specs in ILE RPG programs that reference externally described database files. This is because the ILE RPG compiler still uses the I-spec to define input fields from files.

Very few new functions have been added to the I-spec. Most obvious are the changes required to accommodate 10-character file, record, and field names; larger field lengths and new data types; and the availability of two positions for the number of decimal digits. For program-described files, the ability to specify the format and separator character has been added for the new date and time data type fields. While adjusting to these changes is simple, understanding other changes requires some education.

As discussed in Chapter 6, data structures, data structure subfields, and named constants are no longer defined in I-specs. Their definitions are in the new D-specs. The only time you should need to use I-specs is when you have to work with program-described data or you need to override externally described field names. Most often this happens because you are working with old programs that were never changed to take advantage of externally described files. Of course, there are those special programs that need to work with program-described files, but they're probably few in number. You may also need the I-spec for overriding externally described file descriptions. For example, if you want to use the RPG cycle control-break handling capabilities, you need to define control-break indicators with the I-spec.

The remainder of this chapter is divided into two major sections—using the I-spec to define program-described files, and using the I-spec to override externally described file descriptions.

PROGRAM-DESCRIBED FILES

The I-spec for program-described files can be divided into two general formats—record layout and field layout. For the record layout, record identification entries (positions 7 through 46) describe the input record and its relationship to other records in the file. Figure 7.1 shows the I-spec for record description entries. For the field layout, field description entries (positions 31 through 74) describe the fields in a record. Each field is described on a separate line, below its corresponding record identification entry. Figure 7.2 shows the format of the field description entries. Tables 7.1 and 7.2 summarize changes to record and field description I-specs for program-described files.

Figure 7.1: Record Description Entries

```
*. 1 ...+... 2 ...+... 3 ...+... 4 ...+... 5 ...+... 6 ...+... 7 ...+... 8 ...+... 9 ...+... 10
IFilename++SqNORiPos1+NCCPos2+NCCPos3+NCC................................Comments+++++++++++++
```

Figure 7.2: Field Description Entries

```
*. 1 ...+... 2 ...+... 3 ...+... 4 ...+... 5 ...+... 6 ...+... 7 ...+... 8 ...+... 9 ...+... 10
I.......................Fmt+SPFrom+To+++DcField++++++++++L1M1FrPlMnZr....Comments+++++++++++++
```

Table 7.1: Changes to Program-described Record Identification Entries

RPG/400 Positions	Description	ILE RPG Positions
7 through 14	File name	7 through 16
14 through 16	Logical relationship	16 through 18
15 and 16	Sequence checking	17 and 18
17	Number	19
18	Option	20
19 and 20	Record identifying indicator	21 and 22
21 through 24	Position 1	23 through 27
28 through 31	Position 2	31 through 35
35 through 38	Position 3	39 through 43
25	Not 1	28
26	Code 1	29
27	Character 1	30
32	Not 2	36
33	Code 2	37
34	Character 2	38
39	Not 3	44
40	Code 3	45
41	Character 3	46
75 through 80	Comments	81 through 100

Table 7.2: Changes to Program-described Field Description Entries

RPG/400 Position	Description	ILE Position
N/A	External date/time format	31 through 34
N/A	Date/time separator character	35
43	External data format	36
44 through 47	From position	7 through 41
48 through 51	To position	42 through 46
52	Decimal position	47 and 48
53 through 58	Field name	49 through 62
59 and 60	Control-level indicator	63 and 64
61 and 62	Matching record indicator	65 and 66
63 and 64	Field record relation indicator	67 and 68
65 and 66	Positive field	69 and 70
67 and 68	Negative field	71 and 72
69 and 70	Zero field indicator	73 and 74
75 through 80	Comments	81 through 100

Besides the general format change, there are four changes to the field entry I-spec for program-described files.

♦ Expanded file name (up to 10 characters)

♦ Expanded record length (up to 99,999 bytes)

♦ External date/time format specifier

♦ Date/time separator character

Figure 7.3 illustrates these differences with specifications for a program-described file given for RPG/400 and ILE RPG.

Figure 7.3: Program-described File Input Specifications

RPG/400

```
*. 1 ...+... 2 ...+... 3 ...+... 4 ...+... 5 ...+... 6 ...+... 7 ...+.
IFilenameSqNORiPos1NCCPos2NCCPos3NCC...........................
IARTRAN  NS 01   1 CA
I        OR 02   1 CC
I.................................PFromTo++DFldnmeL1M1FrPlMnZr.
I                               1   1 TRCODE
I                               2  80TRCUST
I                               9  16 TRDATE
I                             P 17  212TRAMT
```

ILE RPG

```
*. 1 ...+... 2 ...+... 3 ...+... 4 ...+... 5 ...+... 6 ...+... 7 ...+.
IFilename++SqNORiPos1+NCCPos2+NCCPos3+NCC.......................
IARTRAN    NS 01   1 CA
I          OR 02   1 CC
I.....................Fmt+SPFrom+To+++DcField++++++++L1M1FrPlMnZr..
I                               1   1  TRCODE
I                               2   8 0TRCUST
I                        *MDY/D 9  16  TRDATE
I                             P 17  21 2TRAMT
```

The example in Figure 7.3 assigns record identifying indicator 01 to records with the character A in position 1 and record identifying indicator 02 to records with the character C in position 1.

In the RPG/400 example, the field TRDATE is defined as a character field with a length of eight. In the ILE RPG example, the definition of this field is modified by adding *MDY in positions 31 through 34 to denote an external date/time type of MMDDYY, a forward slash in position 35 to indicate the date/time separator character, and a D in position 36 to define the date data type. These additions define the field TRDATE as a date field in MMDDYY format with a forward slash as the separator character.

ILE RPG now directly supports date (D), time (T), and time-stamp (Z) data types. *DMY, *YMD, *JUL, *HMS, and several other formats can be specified.

EXTERNALLY DESCRIBED FILES

Except for positioning and the ability to specify 10-character record format and field names, the RPG/400 and ILE RPG I-spec record and field layouts are identical for externally described files. The I-spec for externally described files can also be divided into general formats: record layout and field layout.

Use I-specs with externally described files to change the name of a field or to add RPG functionality, such as a level break or matching records indicator. This may be at the record level or at the field level. With externally described files, the I-spec is only used to override the information that is already defined in the external file. For example, you can rename a field or add a control break indicator to a field.

Record identification entries (positions 7 through 16, and 21 to 22) identify the externally described record format to which ILE RPG functions are added. The format of the record description entries is shown in Figure 7.4.

Figure 7.4: Externally Described Record Format

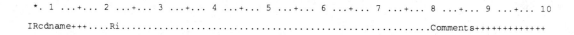

```
*.  1 ...+... 2 ...+... 3 ...+... 4 ...+... 5 ...+... 6 ...+... 7 ...+... 8 ...+... 9 ...+... 10
IRcdname+++....Ri.........................................................Comments++++++++++++
```

Field description entries (positions 21 through 30, 49 through 66, and 69 through 74) describe the ILE RPG functions to be added to the fields in the record. Field description entries are written on the lines following the corresponding record identification entries.

Figure 7.5 shows the format of the field description entries. Tables 7.3 and 7.4 summarize the changes to I-specs for externally described files.

Figure 7.5: ILE RPG Field Description Entries

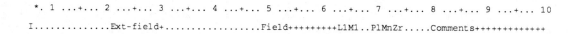

```
*.  1 ...+... 2 ...+... 3 ...+... 4 ...+... 5 ...+... 6 ...+... 7 ...+... 8 ...+... 9 ...+... 10
I..............Ext-field+.................Field++++++++L1M1..P1MnZr.....Comments++++++++++++
```

Table 7.3: Changes to Externally Described Record Identification Entries

RPG/400 Positions	ILE RPG Positions	Name	Entry	Description
6	6	Form type	I	Identification for an input specification.
7 through 14	7 through 16	Record name	Record format name	The RPG/400 name of the record format. A file name can not be used.
15 through 18	N/A	Sequence	Blank	These positions must be blank.
19 and 20	21 and 22	Record ID indicators	Blank	No record identifying indicator.
			01 through 99	General indicator.
			L1 through L9, LR	Control-level indicator used for record identifying indicator.
			H1 through H9	Halt indicator.
			U1 through U8	External indicator.
			RT	Return indicator.
21 through 41	N/A	Record ID code	Blank	Record format names are used to determine the record types used in the program.
42 through 74	N/A	N/A	Blank	N/A
75 through 80	80 through 100	N/A	Optional	This space is available for comments.

Table 7.4: Changes to Externally Described Field Identification Entries

RPG/400 Positions	ILE RPG Positions	Name	Entry	Description
7 through 20	7 through 20	N/A	Blank	N/A
21 through 30	21 through 30	External field name	Field name	If a field within a record in an externally described field is to be renamed, enter the external name of the field in these positions.
31 through 52	31 through 48	N/A	Blank	N/A
53 through 58	49 through 62	RPG/400 field name	Field name	The name of the field as it appears in the external record description (if six characters or less) or the field name that replaces the externally defined field name in positions 21 through 30.
59 and 60	63 and 64	Control level	Blank	This field is a control field.
			L1 through L9	This field is a control field.
61 and 62	65 and 66	Match fields	Blank	Field is not a match field.
			M1 through M9	The field is a match field.
63 and 64	67 and 68	N/A	Blank	N/A

RPG/400 Positions	ILE RPG Positions	Name	Entry	Description
65 through 70	69 through 74	Field indicators	Blank	No indicator specified.
			01 through 99	General indicators.
			H1 through H9	Halt indicators.
			U1 through U8	External indicators.
			RT	Return indicators.
71 through 74	75 through 80	N/A	Blank	N/A
75 through 80	80 through 100	N/A	Optional	This space is available for comments.

Programmers often disagree about whether or not the RPG logic cycle should be used. Without getting into a debate about it, letting the RPG cycle inform your program of control breaks can be advantageous. Figure 7.6 illustrates how control-level indicators are assigned in RPG/400 and how to assign them in ILE RPG.

Figure 7.6: Defining Control-level Indicators in ILE RPG

RPG/400

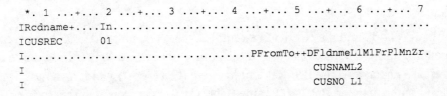

```
*. 1 ...+... 2 ...+... 3 ...+... 4 ...+... 5 ...+... 6 ...+... 7
IRcdname+....In...................................................
ICUSREC    01
I.......................................PFromTo++DFldnmeL1M1FrPlMnZr.
I                                       CUSNAML2
I                                       CUSNO L1
```

ILE RPG

```
*. 1 ...+... 2 ...+... 3 ...+... 4 ...+... 5 ...+... 6 ...+... 7
IRcdname+++....Ri.......................................................
ICUSREC        01
I......................Fmt+SPFrom+To+++DcField++++++++L1M1FrPlMnZr..
I                                      CUSNAM        L2
I                                      CUSNO         L1
```

If you use the Convert RPG Source (CVTRPGSRC) command to convert your RPG/400 source code to ILE RPG, any control-level indicators used to override externally described fields are converted for you. Field names with lengths that exceed 6 characters no longer need to be renamed because ILE RPG supports 10-character field names. But, if you still want to rename a field, Figure 7.7 presents an example of how to do so.

Figure 7.7: Renaming Externally Described Fields

RPG/400

```
*. 1 ...+... 2 ...+... 3 ...+... 4 ...+... 5 ...+... 6 ...+... 7
IRcdname+....In......................................................
ISREC
I.............Ext-field+.....................Field+L1M1..PlMnZr.
I            COST                             CUCOST
```

ILE RPG

```
*. 1 ...+... 2 ...+... 3 ...+... 4 ...+... 5 ...+... 6 ...+... 7
IRcdname+++....Ri.....................................................
ISREC
I.............Ext-field+.................Field++++++++L1M1..PlMnZr..
I            COST                         Cust_cost
```

In both the RPG/400 and the ILE RPG examples, the external field COST is given a more meaningful field name. Because of the ability to define a longer field name and use lowercase characters, the ILE RPG field name (Cust_cost) yields a more meaningful name than the RPG/400 name (CUCOST). You can also rename externally described fields globally with the new PREFIX keyword used in the F-spec. (See Chapter 5 if you need a refresher.)

SUMMARY

By now, you should see that little change has occurred in the I-spec when it comes to defining program-described and externally described files. The significance of the changes to the I-specs is not in what has been added, but in what has been taken away. The main purpose of the ILE RPG I-spec is to describe file data. Most files are externally defined—and the compiler creates the I-specs for these types of files—so you won't be creating very many I-specs. You'll only use them when there's a need to work with program-described files or to override externally described fields.

Chapter 8

Calculation Specification (C-spec)

Calculation specifications (C-specs) have undergone major modification in ILE
RPG. Many changes were required to accommodate relaxed limits in ILE RPG,
while other changes provide substantial usability improvements.

Figures 8.1 and 8.2 show that—with ILE RPG—factor 1, factor 2, and the result field
have all been increased to 14 characters to handle 10-character symbolic names, with
extra space for an array index when needed.

Figure 8.1: Example RPG/400 C-spec

```
 *. 1 ...+... 2 ...+... 3 ...+... 4 ...+... 5 ...+... 6 ...+... 7
C           ITEMNO     CHAINITMREC                    99
C           *IN99      IFEQ *OFF
C                      SUB  1         ITQOH
C                      UPDATITMREC
C                      ENDIF
```

Other changes are also apparent. The operation code has been increased to six
characters. For example, UPDAT has been changed to UPDATE. The five-character
operation codes no longer work in C-specs. Table 8.1 summarizes changes to
operation codes.

Figure 8.2: Example ILE RPG C-spec

```
*. 1 ...+... 2 ...+... 3 ...+... 4 ...+... 5 ...+... 6 ...+... 7 ...+... 8
C     ITEMNO      CHAIN     ITMREC                              99
C     *IN99       IFEQ      *OFF
C                 SUB       1             ITQOH
C                 UPDATE    ITMREC
C                 ENDIF
```

Table 8.1: Renamed and Expanded Operation Codes

RPG/400	ILE RPG
BITOF	BITOFF
CHEKR	CHECKR
COMIT	COMMIT
DEFN	DEFINE
DELET	DELETE
EXCPT	EXCEPT
LOKUP	LOOKUP
OCUR	OCCUR
REDPE	READPE
RETRN	RETURN
SELEC	SELECT
SETOF	SETOFF
UNLCK	UNLOCK
UPDAT	UPDATE
WHxx	WHENxx

The operation extender has been moved to follow the operation code and must be enclosed in parentheses. Operation extenders include H for half adjust, N for read with no lock, and P for pad with blanks.

As in I-specs, decimal positions up to 30 are now supported in C-specs. In Figures 8.3 and 8.4, the number of decimal positions for the field RATIO has been modified from 9 to 15. The length has been modified from 19 to 23.

Figure 8.3: Numeric Field Definition in RPG/400

```
*. 1 ...+... 2 ...+... 3 ...+... 4 ...+... 5 ...+... 6 ...+... 7
C          COST     DIV AMOUNT    RATIO 199
```

Figure 8.4: Numeric Field Definition in ILE RPG

```
*. 1 ...+... 2 ...+... 3 ...+... 4 ...+... 5 ...+... 6 ...+... 7 ...+... 8
C    COST          DIV        AMOUNT        RATIO          2315
```

Only a single conditioning indicator is permitted. If you have old code that uses more than one conditioning indicator, the RPG/400-to-ILE RPG source-conversion utility automatically puts each indicator in a separate statement, as shown in Figures 8.5 and 8.6.

Figure 8.5: Multiple Conditioning Indicators in RPG/400

```
*. 1 ...+... 2 ...+... 3 ...+... 4 ...+... 5 ...+... 6 ...+... 7
C   71 72 73        ADD  1       QOH
```

Figure 8.6: Multiple Conditioning Indicators in ILE RPG

```
*. 1 ...+... 2 ...+... 3 ...+... 4 ...+... 5 ...+... 6 ...+... 7 ...+... 8
C   71
CAN 72
CAN 73           ADD       1          QOH
```

FREE-FORM ARITHMETIC EXPRESSIONS

ILE RPG supports free-form expressions in C-specs. Instead of having to code a complex formula a single step at a time, the new EVAL operation code can be used with an extended factor 2. Standard arithmetic operators supported include:

♦   Addition (+)

♦   Subtraction (-)

♦   Multiplication (*)

♦   Division (/)

♦   Exponentiation (**)

Factor 1 must be blank. For numeric arithmetic operations, you may specify half adjust as an operation extender to round out the result. While conditioning indicators may be used, they should be avoided if possible, as with all C-specs. If you are using control-level indicators, use a single control-level indicator in the C-specs to control the execution of a subroutine instead of having control-level indicators on multiple statements. Because RPG is not an indicator-optimized compiler, indicators should be referenced as little as possible.

Blanks can be freely interspersed between operands and operators to make the code easier to understand. In some cases, blanks are required—for example, to differentiate between exponentiation and multiplication of a reserved word beginning with an asterisk (*). Consider the following expression:

```
AMT**TIME
```

This expression is interpreted as the field AMT raised to the power of the field TIME. If instead you want to multiply AMT by the ILE RPG reserved word *TIME, the expression should be coded in one of these two ways:

```
AMT* *TIME

AMT * *TIME
```

Look at the examples in Figures 8.7 and 8.8. In the first example, the field OECOST is computed as the value of the field OEQTY times the field IMPRIC. In ILE RPG, the half-adjust operation extender has been enclosed in parentheses and moved next to the operation code.

Figure 8.7: Fixed Calculation Expressions in RPG/400

```
*. 1 ...+... 2 ...+... 3 ...+... 4 ...+... 5 ...+... 6 ...+... 7
* Example 1
C           OEQTY     MULT IMPRIC     OECOST     H
*
* Example 2
C           OEQTY     MULT IMWGHT     OEWGHT
C                     ADD  PKWGHT     OEWGHT
*
* Example 3
C           OECOST    SUB  OEDISC     XXCOST
C           XXCOST    MULT STTAX      OESTAX
```

Figure 8.8: Free-form Calculation Expressions in ILE RPG

```
*. 1 ...+... 2 ...+... 3 ...+... 4 ...+... 5 ...+... 6 ...+... 7 ...+... 8
* Example 1
C                     EVAL(H)   OECOST = OEQTY * IMPRIC
*
* Example 2
C                     EVAL      OEWGHT = (OEQTY * IMWGHT) + PKWGHT
*
* Example 3
C                     EVAL      OESTAX = (OECOST - OEDISC) * STTAX
```

The second sample is a two-part calculation. The field OEWGHT is computed as the value of the field OEQTY times the field IMWGHT, with the field PKWGHT added to the result. Based upon the rules of precedence, the use of parentheses in the ILE RPG version is optional. The order of precedence for arithmetic operations in ILE RPG free-form expressions is as follows:

♦ Parentheses

♦ Built-in functions

♦ Unary +, unary -, NOT

♦ Exponentiation

♦ Multiplication and division

♦ Addition and subtraction

In the last example, the field OESTAX is computed as the value of the field OECOST minus the field OEDISC, with the field STTAX multiplied by the result. The parentheses in Figure 8.8 are required. Without them, the field OEDISC would be multiplied by the field STTAX and the result would be subtracted from the field OECOST, yielding erroneous results.

When using ILE RPG, you may want to use parentheses to make your code more readable, even if they are not required. Some complex formulas can require several lines of code. Sometimes it's convenient to break up code into several lines to make it more readable. Figures 8.9 and 8.10 illustrate this concept.

Figure 8.9: Calculation Expression in RPG/400

```
*. 1 ...+... 2 ...+... 3 ...+... 4 ...+... 5 ...+... 6 ...+... 7
C           TMSFT1    MULT EMRATE    TMPAY
 *
C           EMRATE    ADD  EMPRE2    XRATE
C           TMSFT2    MULT XRATE     XWAGET
C                     ADD  XWAGET    TMPAY
 *
C           EMRATE    ADD  EMPRE3    XRATE
C           TMSFT3    MULT XRATE     XWAGET
C                     ADD  XWAGET    TMPAY
```

Figure 8.10: Calculation Expression in ILE RPG

```
*. 1 ...+... 2 ...+... 3 ...+... 4 ...+... 5 ...+... 6 ...+... 7 ...+... 8
C                EVAL      TMPAY = TMSFT1 * EMRATE
C                              + (EMRATE + EMPRE2) * TMSFT2
 *
C                              + (EMRATE + EMPRE3) * TMSFT3
```

As an example, let's say we want to compute the total of first-, second-, and third-shift pay. The shift premium must be added in before multiplying the rate times the hours. Figure 8.10 shows how to replace seven RPG/400 calculations with a single ILE RPG expression.

If the field TMPAY is not large enough to hold the result, a numeric overflow exception occurs and the status code in the program status data structure is set to 103. This produces a run-time halt unless a *PSSR subroutine is defined in the program, in which case the *PSSR subroutine is called. If numeric overflow occurs in ILE RPG in arithmetic operations that do not involve expressions, such as Z-ADD, truncation without a halt occurs just as it does in RPG/400. Specifying TRUNCNBR(*NO) when compiling an ILE RPG program forces a run-time halt any time numeric overflow occurs.

CONTINUED LITERALS

The ILE RPG example in Figure 8.11 contains two expressions with continued literals. The first uses a plus sign (+) continuation character, which means the literal is continued with the first non-blank character in positions 36 through 80 of the next line. The second example uses a hyphen continuation character, which means the literal is continued in position 36 of the next line even if it contains a blank. The fields DES1 and DES2 both have the same value.

Figure 8.11: Literal Continuations

```
*. 1 ...+... 2 ...+... 3 ...+... 4 ...+... 5 ...+... 6 ...+... 7 ...+... 8
C                   EVAL      DES1 = 'Notice the difference between plus +
C                                    sign and hyphen continuation for +
C                                    literals.'
C                   EVAL      DES2 = 'Notice the difference between plus -
C                                    sign and hyphen continuation for literals.'
```

An expression can be continued over multiple lines. Continued lines must be blank in positions 7 through 35. No special continuation character is required unless a literal is being continued.

Commented lines with an asterisk in position 7 can be interspersed between continued lines. Blank lines can also be used.

FREE-FORM LOGICAL EXPRESSIONS

In addition to the EVAL operation, ILE RPG also supports free-form expressions for the DOU, DOW, IF, and WHEN operations. These operations are functionally equivalent to the DOUxx, DOWxx, IFxx, and WHENxx operations except, instead of comparing factor 1 to factor 2, the extended factor 2 entry is used for the comparison. Valid operators include:

♦   Equal to (=)

♦   Greater than or equal to (>=)

♦   Greater than (>)

♦   Less than or equal to (<=)

♦   Less than (<)

♦   Not equal (<>)

Figures 8.12 and 8.13 show the difference between *do while* loops in RPG/400 and ILE RPG.

Figure 8.12: The Do While Loop in RPG/400

```
 *. 1 ...+... 2 ...+... 3 ...+... 4 ...+... 5 ...+... 6 ...+... 7
C           X           DOWLT50
C           IN,X        ANDNE*BLANKS
C                       MOVE  IN,X        OUT,Y
C                       ADD   1           X
C                       ADD   1           Y
C                       ENDDO
```

Figure 8.13: The Do While Loop in ILE RPG

```
 *. 1 ...+... 2 ...+... 3 ...+... 4 ...+... 5 ...+... 6 ...+... 7 ...+... 8
C                       DOW         Y < 50 AND IN(X) <> ' '
C                       MOVE        IN(X)        OUT(Y)
C                       ADD         1            X
C                       ADD         1            Y
C                       ENDDO
```

In each of these examples, two conditions must be true for the loop to continue. First, Y must be less than 50. Second, the specified element (indexed by X) of the array IN must not be blank. As long as both of these tests are true, the loop continues. If either test is not true, the loop ends. The ILE RPG example combines both of these tests into a single DOW statement with the tests separated by an AND operator.

Complex expressions can be constructed using the AND and OR operators. How do you know the difference between the field OR and the operation OR? You might not know at first, but the compiler does. While variables named AND and OR are valid in ILE RPG, they should be avoided to prevent misunderstanding.

Control-level and conditioning indicators may be used. Factor 1 must be blank. No operation extenders are permitted.

The RPG/400 example in Figure 8.14 is a little more complex than the previous examples. It uses multiple WHxx operations within a SELEC group. The first WHEQ operation tests for TRCODE equal to A while the second tests for TRCODE equal to C or D. An appropriate action description padded with blanks is moved to the field ACTION.

Figure 8.14: SELEC/WHxx Operations in RPG/400

```
*. 1 ...+... 2 ...+... 3 ...+... 4 ...+... 5 ...+... 6 ...+... 7
C                    SELEC
C          TRCODE    WHEQ 'A'
C                    MOVEL'ADD'      ACTION      P
C          TRCODE    WHEQ 'C'
C          TRCODE    OREQ 'D'
C                    MOVEL'UPDATE'   ACTION      P
C                    OTHER
C                    MOVEL'ERROR'    ACTION      P
C                    ENDSL
```

The ILE RPG example in Figure 8.15 again combines multiple tests into a single statement using the WHEN operation with the tests separated by an OR. The MOVEL operation has also been changed to an EVAL in this example. Even though half adjust is the only valid operation extender with EVAL, the result is still padded with blanks. That's because when the EVAL operation is used to set the value of a character field, it functions the same as a MOVEL(P). The result is left-adjusted and padded with blanks on the right. If the expression is longer than the variable, the value is truncated with no error given.

Figure 8.15: SELECT/WHEN Operations in ILE RPG

```
*. 1 ...+... 2 ...+... 3 ...+... 4 ..+... 5 ...+... 6 ...+... 7 ...+... 8
C                    SELECT
C                    WHEN      TRCODE = 'A'
C                    EVAL      ACTION = 'ADD'
C                    WHEN      TRCODE = 'C' OR TRCODE = 'D'
C                    EVAL      ACTION = 'UPDATE'
C                    OTHER
C                    EVAL      ACTION = 'ERROR'
C                    ENDSL
```

Sometimes intermediate results must be calculated to perform a test. When doing a credit check on an order, you add the order amount to the customer's Accounts Receivable balance and compare the sum to the customer's credit limit. This requires two separate operations in RPG/400 (Figure 8.16) where as ILE RPG requires only a single statement (Figure 8.17).

Figure 8.16: IF Statement in RPG/400

```
*. 1 ...+... 2 ...+... 3 ...+... 4 ...+... 5 ...+... 6 ...+... 7
C           EOCOST    ADD  CMBAL      XCHECK
C           XCHECK    IFGT CMCRED
C                     MOVE 'N'        OEOKAY
C                     ENDIF
```

Figure 8.17: IF Statement in ILE RPG

```
*. 1 ...+... 2 ...+... 3 ...+... 4 ...+... 5 ...+... 6 ...+... 7 ...+... 8
C                     IF        OECOST + CMBAL > CMCRED
C                     MOVE      'N'         OEOKAY
C                     ENDIF
```

Figure 8.17 shows that the IF operation supports arithmetic expressions as part of the extended factor 2 in ILE RPG. The field OECOST is first added to the field CMBAL and the sum compared to the field CMCRED. Comparison operators such as greater than have a lower order of precedence than arithmetic operators. Consequently, the arithmetic is done first, followed by the comparison. If AND or OR is used, the logical operations are performed last because they are lowest in order of precedence. Table 8.2 summarizes the changes to C-specs in ILE RPG.

Table 8.2: Summary of Changes to C-Specs

RPG/400 Position	Description	ILE RPG Position
7 and 8	Control level	7 and 8
9 through 17	Conditioning indicators	9 through 11
18 through 27	Factor 1	12 through 25
28 through 32	Operation code	26 through 35

RPG/400 Position	Description	ILE RPG Position
33 through 42	Factor 2	36 through 49
43 through 48	Result field	50 through 63
49 through 51	Field length	64 through 68
52	Decimal positions	69 and 70
53	Operation extender	26 through 35
54 and 55	Hi/no record found indicator	71 and 72
56 and 57	Low/error indicator	73 and 74
58 and 59	Equal/end-of-file	75 and 76
N/A	Extended factor 2	36 through 76
60 through 74	Comments	81 through 100

SUMMARY

Many of the changes made to C-specs give you better control over the logic of your programs. The expanded operation codes make C-specs more readable. The new EVAL, DOU, DOW, IF, and WHEN operations, and the introduction of expressions to C-specs, provide even more usability improvements to ILE RPG.

Chapter 9

Output Specification (O-spec)

Output specifications (O-specs) describe the format of a record in a program-described output file. Many of the changes to O-specs in ILE RPG are very similar to the types of changes that were made to accommodate the I-specs. The examples in Figures 9.1 and 9.2 demonstrate some of the differences between RPG/400 and ILE RPG O-specs when coding a program-described disk file.

Figure 9.1: RPG/400 O-spec Disk File Example

```
*. 1 ...+... 2 ...+... 3 ...+... 4 ...+... 5 ...+... 6 ...+... 7
OName++++DFBASbSaN01N02N03Excnam...............................
OITEM01PFEADD           ADDITM

O...............N01N02N03Field+YBEnd+PConstant/editword++++++++
O                       ITNUM     2P
O                       ITDESC    42
O                       ITAMT     46P
```

Expanded space is provided to support ending positions up to 99,999 and names for 10-character files, record formats, fields, and except labels. Unlike C-specs, all three conditioning indicators have been retained in O-specs.

Figure 9.2: ILE RPG O-spec Disk File Example

```
*. 1 ...+... 2 ...+... 3 ...+... 4 ...+... 5 ...+... 6 ...+... 7 ...+... 8
OFilename++DF..N01N02N03Excnam++++B++A++Sb+Sa+...........................
OITEM01PF  EADD        ADDITM

O.............N01N02N03Field++++++++YB.End++PConstant/editword/DTformat+
O                      ITNUM            2P
O                      ITDESC           42
O                      ITAMT            46P
```

Figures 9.3 and 9.4 show some of the changes in O-specs for coding program-described printer files.

Figure 9.3: RPG/400 O-spec Printer File Example

```
*. 1 ...+... 2 ...+... 3 ...+... 4 ...+... 5 ...+... 6 ...+... 7
OName++++DFBASbSaN01N02N03Excnam...............................
OQSYSPRT E 3
O        E 21

O.............N01N02N03Field+YBEnd+PConstant/editword+++++++
O                     ITNUM 3    5
O                     ITDESC   50
O                     ITAMT 3   65
O                               93 'This is a long constant'
O                              113 'which spans several'
O                              120 'lines.'
```

Figure 9.4: ILE RPG O-spec Printer File Example

```
*. 1 ...+... 2 ...+... 3 ...+... 4 ...+... 5 ...+... 6 ...+... 7 ...+... 8
OFilename++DF..N01N02N03Excnam++++B++A++Sb+Sa+...........................
OQSYSPRT   E                5 1

O.............N01N02N03Field++++++++YB.End++PConstant/editword/DTformat+
O                      ITNUM         3    5
O                      ITDESC           50
O                      ITAMT         3   65
O                                       120 'This is a long constant +
O                                           which spans several +
O                                           lines.'
```

RPG/400 only supports zero to three "space before" or "space after" lines. The RPG/400 example in Figure 9.2 requires two exception output statements to space five lines before printing—one statement to space three lines and another to space two lines.

The ILE RPG example in Figure 9.4 requires only a single line because values from 0 to 255 are supported for space before and space after lines. In addition, "skip before" and "skip after" line numbers can now range from 0 to 255.

Constants or edit words can be continued on multiple lines in positions 53 to 80. The line being continued must end with a plus sign or a hyphen. A plus sign means continuation starts with the first non-blank character in or past position 53 of the next line. A hyphen means continuation starts in position 53 of the next line even if position 53 is blank. The continuation line must contain an O in position 6 and be blank in positions 7 through 52. Blank separator lines and comment lines are permitted between continued lines. Table 9.1 summarizes changes to O-specs.

Table 9.1: Differences between RPG/400 and ILE RPG O-specs

RPG/400 Position	Description	ILE RPG Position
7 through 14	File name or record format name	7 through 16
14 through 16	Logical relationship	16 through 18
15	Type	17
15	Type	17
16	Fetch overflow	18
17	Space before	40 through 42
18	Space after	43 through 45
19 and 20	Skip before	46 through 48
21 and 22	Skip after	49 through 51
23 through 31	Output indicators	21 through 29
32 through 37	Except name	30 through 39

RPG/400 Position	Description	ILE RPG Position
32 through 37	Field name	30 through 43
38	Edit code	44
39	Blank after	45
40 through 43	End position	47 through 51
44	Data format	52
45 through 70	Constant or edit word	53 through 80
75 through 80	Comment	81 through 100

SUMMARY

The differences between the O-specs in RPG/400 and those of ILE RPG are not drastic. The major differences are changes to accommodate 10-character file and field names, the continuation of literals and edit words, and support for larger space before and after values.

Chapter 10

Built-in Functions

Built-in functions perform specific types of operations on data. ILE RPG has several new built-in functions that operate similarly to those found in CL. In fact, if you already have an understanding of CL functions it will help you understand ILE RPG built-in functions. For example, in CL, %SST performs a substring function, %BIN provides a binary conversion, and %SWITCH tests job switches. Similar functions are available in ILE RPG.

Built-in functions in ILE RPG begin with a percent sign (%) and are followed by one or more arguments enclosed in parentheses. In ILE RPG, multiple arguments are separated by a colon. This is consistent with other keywords in ILE RPG. One of the minor differences between CL functions and ILE RPG functions is that CL uses a blank as a delimiter for arguments while ILE RPG requires a colon.

Built-in functions are supported in D-specs in the keyword entry in positions 44 through 80. Only compile-time values can be used for arguments in these positions. Variables that are computed at run time can not be used in an argument. When used in conjunction with the keywords DIM, OCCURS, OVERLAY, and PERRCD, all arguments must be defined previously in the program.

C-specs also support built-in functions in the extended factor 2 entry. Free-form expressions can be used as the argument of a built-in function and may include other built-in functions. Unlike operation codes, built-in functions return a value rather than placing a value in a result field.

So what does a built-in function really do? Let's compare the substring built-in function in CL, RPG/400, and ILE RPG.

USING A SUBSTRING TO RETRIEVE A STRING

The substring built-in function in CL can be used to retrieve or modify a portion of a character string contained in a CL character variable or in the local data area. Either %SST or %SUBSTRING can be used in an expression or as the VAR or VALUE parameter of the Change Variable (CHGVAR) command. The character variable name (or *LDA), starting position, and length must be specified as arguments. Figure 10.1 shows an example.

Figure 10.1: Using %SST to Retrieve a String in CL

```
DCL        VAR(&BEG) TYPE(*CHAR) LEN(6) VALUE('ABCDE')
DCL        VAR(&END) TYPE(*CHAR) LEN(8) VALUE('XXXXXXX')
CHGVAR     VAR(&END) VALUE(%SST(&BEG 2 4))
```

In the CL sample in Figure 10.1, four characters are extracted from the variable &BEG, starting in position 2. The variable &END contains a value of 'BCDE' if the variable &BEG has the value 'ABCDEF'. Because it exceeds the number of characters in the substring, the variable &END is automatically padded with blanks.

RPG/400 and ILE RPG support the substring operation in C-specs. The character variable from which a value is to be extracted is specified in factor 2. The start position can optionally be specified in factor 2 following the variable. A colon separates these two elements in factor 2. If not specified, the start position defaults to 1. The length to be extracted can optionally be specified in factor 1. If not specified, it defaults to the length of the string from the start position. The variable to contain the substring is specified in the result field.

In the RPG/400 sample in Figure 10.2, four characters are extracted from the variable BEG starting in position 2. The variable END contains the value 'BCDE' if the variable BEG has the value 'ABCDEF'. Because the length of the variable END is greater than the substring length, the operation extender P is specified to pad with blanks. ILE RPG supports the SUBST operation code, which is identical in function to the RPG/400 version.

Figure 10.2: Using SUBST to Retrieve a String in RPG/400

```
*. 1 ...+... 2 ...+... 3 ...+... 4 ...+... 5 ...+... 6 ...+... 7
CL0N01N02N03Factor1+++OpcdeFactor2+++ResultLenDHHiLoEqComments+++
C                    MOVE 'ABCDEF'  BEG       6
C                    MOVE 'XXXXXXXX'END       8
C            4       SUBSTBEG:2     END         P
```

In contrast, the ILE RPG example in Figure 10.3 uses the substring built-in function and compares closely to the CL sample. %SUBST is used in ILE RPG instead of the %SST or %SUBSTRING used in CL. A colon is used to separate the variable, start position, and length arguments, instead of the blank used in CL.

Figure 10.3: Using %SUBST to Retrieve a String in ILE RPG

```
*. 1 ...+... 2 ...+... 3 ...+... 4 ...+... 5 ...+... 6 ...+... 7 ...+.
CL0N01Factor1+++++++Opcode&ExtExtended-factor2++++++++++++++++++++++++++
C                    EVAL      BEG = 'ABCDEF'
C                    EVAL      END = 'XXXXXXXX'
C                    EVAL      END = %SUBST(BEG:2:4)
```

Even though the operation extender P is not specified (and can not be specified with the EVAL operation code), the variable END still has the value 'BCDE'. When used with character fields, the EVAL operation functions similarly to a MOVEL(P). When using the substring built-in function, padding with blanks is implied with the EVAL operation in ILE RPG as it is with the CHGVAR command in CL.

USING A SUBSTRING TO MODIFY A STRING

The previous substring examples were used to retrieve a substring. Let's take a look at how to change a substring.

While the SUBST operation code has proved valuable in RPG/400, it is limited because it only allows you to retrieve a substring, not to modify one. Although the substring operation has the same restriction in ILE RPG, the EVAL operation code allows you to overcome the limitation.

A substring can be modified in CL by using the substring built-in function in the VAR parameter of the CHGVAR command. In the CL example in Figure 10.4, part of the variable &MOD (starting in position 3 and extending for a length of two characters) is replaced with the value of the variable &CON. Even though the length of the variable &CON is longer than two, only the first two characters are used. Upon execution of the CHGVAR, the value of the variable &MOD changes to 'VWabZ'.

Figure 10.4: Using %SST to Modify a String in CL

```
DCL        VAR(&MOD) TYPE(*CHAR) LEN(5) VALUE('VWXYZ')
DCL        VAR(&CON) TYPE(*CHAR) LEN(5) VALUE('abcde')
CHGVAR     VAR(%SST(&MOD 3 2)) VALUE(&CON)
```

Figure 10.5 shows three substring examples that illustrate a similar capability for ILE RPG. A substring can be changed in ILE RPG using the EVAL operation code with the %SUBST built-in function specified on the left side of the equal sign. The first example is similar to the CL example shown in Figure 10.1. In this case, the value of the variable MOD is changed to 'VWabZ'.

Figure 10.5: Using %SUBST to Modify a String in ILE RPG

```
    *. 1 ...+... 2 ...+... 3 ...+... 4 ...+... 5 ...+... 6 ...+... 7 ...+.
DName++++++++++ETDsFrom+++To/L+++IDc.Keywords+++++++++++++++++++++++++++
D MOD             S              5    INZ('VWXYZ')
D CON             S              5    INZ('abcde')
D START1          S              5  0 INZ(3)
D LENGTH          S              5  0 INZ(2)
D START2          S              5  0 INZ(4)

CL0N01Factor1+++++++Opcode&ExtExtended-factor2+++++++++++++++++++++++++++
 * First example...
C                   EVAL      %SUBST(MOD:3:2) = CON

 * Second example...
C                   EVAL      %SUBST(MOD: 3: 2) = %SUBST(CON: 4: 2)

 * Third example...
C                   EVAL      %SUBST(MOD:START1:LENGTH) =
C                               %SUBST(CON:START:LENGTH)
```

```
* Fourth example...
C                    EVAL      %SUBST(MOD:START1-1:LENGTH) =
C                              %SUBST(CON:START2/2:LENGTH+1)
```

The second ILE RPG example in Figure 10.5 shows the use of the EVAL operation code with the %SUBST built-in function specified on both sides of the equal sign. This permits the value of a substring to be set equal to the value of another substring. The third and fourth characters in the variable MOD are replaced with the fourth and fifth characters of the variable CON. Upon completion of the execution of the EVAL operation, the variable MOD contains a value of 'VWdeZ'.

If desired, blanks can be used between the arguments in a built-in function to make the code more readable. Coding %SUBST(MOD:3:2) is the same as coding %SUBST(MOD: 3: 2).

Variables can be used for the start position and length, as shown in the third ILE example in Figure 10.5. The results are identical to the previous example; that is, the variable MOD has a value of 'VWdeZ'.

Any valid expression is permitted for the start position and length when the %SUBST built-in function is used as a target, as shown in the fourth ILE RPG example. Part of the variable MOD (starting in position 2 and extending for a length of three characters) is replaced with the second, third, and fourth characters from the variable CON. Upon completion of the execution of the EVAL operation, the variable MOD has a value of 'VbcdZ'.

An expression can be continued over multiple lines. Continued lines must be blank in positions 7 through 35. No special continuation character is required unless a literal is being continued.

Run-time errors can occur when using the %SUBST built-in function if the start position is less than or equal to 0, the length is less than zero, or a combination of the start position and length would cause the substring to exceed the length of the field in the first argument. When used as a target, the first argument of the %SUBST built-in function must refer to a storage location. In other words, it must be a field, data structure subfield, array name, array element, or table element.

The ability to use the %SUBST built-in function as a target to change a portion of the value of a field is a substantial improvement to ILE RPG. Think of how much code this would take in RPG/400 if the start position and length were variables versus using one line of code in ILE RPG.

THE TRIM FUNCTION

Several built-in functions are available in ILE RPG to trim blanks from character variables. %TRIMR trims trailing blanks from the right side of a character variable. %TRIML trims leading blanks from the left side of a character variable. %TRIM trims leading and trailing blanks from a character variable.

As illustrated in Table 10.1, the argument of the %TRIMR, %TRIML, and %TRIM built-in functions can specify a character variable or a valid character expression. The plus sign used in conjunction with character variables indicates concatenation (combining), not addition.

Table 10.1: Trim Function Examples

Function	Value	Result
%TRIML	' ILE RPG '	'ILE RPG '
%TRIMR	' ILE RPG '	' ILE RPG'
%TRIM	' ILE RPG '	'ILE RPG'
%TRIML	'ILE RPG'	'ILE RPG'
%TRIMR	'ILE RPG'	'ILE RPG'
%TRIM	'ILE RPG'	'ILE RPG'
%TRIML	' ILE ' + ' RPG '	'ILE RPG '
%TRIMR	' ILE ' + ' RPG '	' ILE RPG'
%TRIM	' ILE ' + ' RPG '	'ILE RPG'

Since the availability of the CAT operation code, concatenating a first name with a last name has been simple, as shown in the RPG/400 sample in Figure 10.6.

Figure 10.6: CAT Operation in RPG/400

```
*. 1 ...+... 2 ...+... 3 ...+... 4 ...+... 5 ...+... 6 ...+... 7
CL0N01N02N03Factor1+++OpcdeFactor2+++ResultLenDHHiLoEqComments+++
C           FIRST     CAT  LAST:1    XNAME       P
```

The field FIRST is concatenated with the field LAST, with one blank in between. The result of the operation is placed in the field XNAME and padded with blanks. If the field FIRST contains the value John and the field LAST contains the value Smith, the field XNAME contains the value John Smith. ILE RPG supports the CAT operation code, which is identical in function to the RPG/400 version; it also can accomplish the concatenation with the built-in trim function as shown in Figure 10.7.

Figure 10.7: %TRIMR Function in ILE RPG

```
*. 1 ...+... 2 ...+... 3 ...+... 4 ...+... 5 ...+... 6 ...+... 7 ...+... 8
CL0N01Factor1+++++++Opcode&ExtExtended-factor2+++++++++++++++++++++++++++++
C                   EVAL      XNAME = %TRIMR(FIRST) + ' ' + LAST
```

The ILE RPG example in Figure 10.7 uses the EVAL operation in conjunction with an expression containing a built-in function. The %TRIMR trims the trailing blanks from the right side of the character variable—in this case, the field FIRST. Because the field XNAME is a character variable, the plus sign signifies concatenation. So the field FIRST with the blanks trimmed from the right is concatenated with a single blank. The result is concatenated with the field LAST. This ILE RPG example in Figure 10.7 yields the same results as the RPG/400 example in Figure 10.6.

Both the CAT operation and the EVAL operation with %TRIMR work well unless there are leading blanks in the first or last name. If the field FIRST contains the value Jane and the field LAST contains the value Doe with two leading blanks, the field XNAME contains the value "Jane   Doe" (with three blanks between Jane and Doe).

The ILE RPG example in Figure 10.8 solves this problem using the %TRIM built-in function, which causes the blanks to be trimmed from both sides of the specified variable. It now makes no difference whether or not the fields FIRST and LAST have leading or trailing blanks.

Figure 10.8: The %TRIM Function in ILE RPG

```
*. 1 ...+... 2 ...+... 3 ...+... 4 ...+... 5 ...+... 6 ...+... 7 ...+... 8
CL0N01Factor1+++++++Opcode&ExtExtended-factor2+++++++++++++++++++++++++++++
C                   EVAL      XNAME = %TRIM(FIRST) + ' ' + %TRIM(LAST)
```

The %TRIM built-in function in ILE RPG reduces the amount of code required to combine two or more fields, while eliminating leading and trailing blanks. ILE RPG requires a single statement to perform the same function that might have been coded as a complex subroutine or a called program in RPG/400.

%ELEM WITH ARRAYS

When arrays are used in RPG/400, the number of elements and the element length and decimal positions must be coded individually in E-specs. This means that, if you need to change the number of elements for these arrays, you have to modify multiple E-specs. In addition, if the number of elements is specified as a literal in factor 2 of DO loops in C-specs, these also have to be modified. Even if you use a variable in factor 2, you still have to modify at least one statement. For example, look at the RPG/400 code in Figure 10.9.

Figure 10.9: Array Processing in RPG/400

```
  *. 1 ...+... 2 ...+... 3 ...+... 4 ...+... 5 ...+... 6 ...+... 7
E....FromfileTofile++Name++N/rN/tbLenPDSArrnamLenPDSComments+++++
E                    TOT1        9   7 2
E                    TOT2        9   7 2
E                    TOT3        9   7 2
  *
CL0N01N02N03Factor1+++OpcdeFactor2+++ResultLenDHHiLoEqComments+++
C          *LIKE     DEFN TOT1       OUT
C                    DO   9          X         50
C                    Z-ADDTOT1,X     OUT
C                    EXCPTPRINT1
C                    ENDDO
C                    DO   9          X
C                    Z-ADDTOT2,X     OUT
C                    EXCPTPRINT1
C                    ENDDO
C                    DO   9          X
C                    Z-ADDTOT3,X     OUT
C                    EXCPTPRINT1
C                    ENDDO
```

The arrays TOT1, TOT2, and TOT3 are all defined with nine elements of seven digits with two decimal positions. If you need to increase the number of elements to 11, you must modify all three E-specs. In addition, you need to modify factor 2 of all three of the DO operations in the C-specs. Now look at the ILE RPG example in Figure 10.10.

Figure 10.10: Array Processing in ILE RPG

```
DName++++++++++ETDsFrom+++To/L+++IDc.Keywords++++++++++++++++++++++++
D TOT1            S                 7  2 DIM(9)
D TOT2            S                        LIKE(TOT1) DIM(%ELEM(TOT1))
D TOT3            S                        LIKE(TOT1) DIM(%ELEM(TOT1))
D OUT             S                        LIKE(TOT1)
D NUMELEM         C                        CONST(%ELEM(TOT1))
D X               S                 5  0
 *
CL0N01Factor1++++++Opcode&ExtFactor2+++++++Result+++++++Len++D+HiLoEq
C                  DO        NUMELEM        X
C                  Z-ADD     TOT1(X)        OUT
C                  EXCEPT    PRINT1
C                  ENDDO
C                  DO        NUMELEM        X
C                  Z-ADD     TOT2(X)        OUT
C                  EXCEPT    PRINT1
C                  ENDDO
C                  DO        NUMELEM        X
C                  Z-ADD     TOT3(X)        OUT
C                  EXCEPT    PRINT1
C                  ENDDO
```

The ILE RPG example requires changing only a single line of code to redimension the arrays. The %ELEM built-in function returns the number of elements in an array. Attributes are coded only for the array TOT1 in the D-specs. The LIKE keyword is used to assign the data type, length, and number of decimal positions for the elements in the arrays TOT2 and TOT3 to be the same as in the array TOT1. The %ELEM built-in function is used on the DIM keyword to cause the arrays TOT2 and TOT3 to have the same number of elements (dimensions) as the array TOT1.

This means that, if you need to modify the number of elements for these arrays, you only need to change the D-spec defining the array TOT1. When you recompile your program, the arrays TOT2 and TOT3 are automatically defined to be the same data type, length, decimal positions, and array dimensions as the array TOT1.

The numeric constant NUMELEM is defined as the value of the number of elements in the array TOT1 using the %ELEM built-in function in D-specs. NUMELEM is coded instead of coding a 9 in factor 2 of the DO loops in C-specs. Now if the number of elements in the arrays changes, no changes are required to C-specs. When the program is recompiled, the numeric constant NUMELEM automatically reflects the new value.

The way the %ELEM built-in function works with tables is similar to the way it is used with arrays. Whenever identically defined arrays or tables are defined in ILE RPG, they should be defined based upon the main array or table using the %ELEM built-in function. Any time an array is used in a DO loop in C-specs, the number of elements should also be coded in factor 2 using the %ELEM built-in function. Using these techniques can improve program maintainability and reduce debugging time.

%ELEM WITH MULTIPLE-OCCURRENCE DATA STRUCTURES

The number of occurrences of a multiple-occurrence data structure is coded in I-specs in RPG/400. When the multiple-occurrence data structure is used in a DO loop in C-specs, the number of occurrences is generally coded in factor 2. This means that, if the number of occurrences changes, you must change multiple lines of code. Take a look at the RPG/400 example in Figure 10.11.

Figure 10.11: Using a Multiple-occurrence Data Structure in RPG/400

```
*. 1 ...+... 2 ...+... 3 ...+... 4 ...+... 5 ...+... 6 ...+... 7
IDsname....NODsExt-file++.............OccrLen+...................
IGLDS        DS                     500
I                                     1   9 GLNUM
I                                    10 182GLAMT
 *
CL0N01N02N03Factor1+++OpcdeFactor2+++ResultLenDHHiLoEqComments+++
C                    DO    500       X        50
C           X        OCUR GLDS
C                    EXCPTPRINT
C                    ENDDO
```

The multiple-occurrence data structure GLDS is defined in I-specs with 500 occurrences. The number 500 is also hard-coded in factor 2 of the DO loop in C-specs. Both specifications have to be modified if the number of occurrences changes. Now take a look at the ILE RPG example in Figure 10.12.

Figure 10.12: Using a Multiple-occurrence Data Structure in ILE RPG

```
*. 1 ...+... 2 ...+... 3 ...+... 4 ...+... 5 ...+... 6 ...+... 7 ...+... 8
DName++++++++++ETDsFrom+++To/L+++IDc.Keywords+++++++++++++++++++++++++++++++
D GLDS          DS                    OCCURS(500)
D  GLNUM                     9
D  GLAMT                     9 2
D  NUMOCC        C                    CONST(%ELEM(GLDS))
```

```
D X               S              5 0
*
CLON01Factor1+++++++Opcode&ExtFactor2+++++++Result++++++++Len++D+HiLoEq....
C                   DO        NUMOCC              X
C         X         OCCUR     GLDS
C                   EXCEPT    PRINT
C                   ENDDO
```

The ILE RPG example requires changing only a single line of code. The %ELEM built-in function returns the number of occurrences in a multiple-occurrence data structure. The OCCURS keyword makes the data structure GLDS a multiple-occurrence data structure with 500 occurrences.

The numeric constant NUMOCC is defined as the value of the number of occurrences in the multiple-occurrence data structure GLDS using the %ELEM built-in function in D-specs. Instead of coding a 500 in factor 2 of the DO loop in C-specs, NUMOCC is coded instead. Now if the number of occurrences in the multiple-occurrence data structure changes, the C-specs require no alteration. When the program is recompiled, the numeric constant NUMOCC automatically reflects the new value. The %ELEM built-in function can be used anywhere a numeric constant is valid within the functions column of the D-specs or the extended factor 2 of the C-specs.

%SIZE BUILT-IN FUNCTION

The %SIZE built-in function returns the number of bytes of storage occupied by a literal, named constant, data structure, data structure subfield, field, array, or table name specified as the first argument.

When used with a character or hexadecimal literal, %SIZE returns the number of bytes occupied by that literal. For numeric literals, the number of digits including leading and trailing zeros is returned.

If %SIZE is used with a numeric variable stored in packed format, the packed length is returned (for example, a seven-digit, packed field returns a size of 4 because it take 4 bytes to store the number in packed format). For binary numbers, the binary length (4 or 2) is returned.

When the first argument of the %SIZE built-in function is an array name or table name, the size of a single element is returned. If a multiple occurrence data structure is used, the size of a single occurrence is returned. If *ALL is specified as the second argument, the sizes of all elements or occurrences are returned.

Figure 10.13 illustrates some examples of values returned when the %SIZE built-in function is used. %SIZE can be used anywhere a numeric constant is valid within the functions column of the D-specs or the extended factor 2 of the C-specs.

Figure 10.13: The %SIZE Function in ILE RPG

```
*. 1 ...+... 2 ...+... 3 ...+... 4 ...+... 5 ...+... 6 ...+... 7 ...+... 8
D PACKNUM         S              13P 4
D BINNUM          S               9B 0
D SIGNNUM         S              15S 0
D CHARVAR         S              40A
D PACKARR         S               5P 0 DIM(10)
D SIGNARR         S               5S 0 DIM(10)
D CHARARR         S              11   DIM(5)
D MULTOCCDS       DS              8   OCCURS(20)
D CHARCON         C                   'abcdefgh'
D NUMCON          C                   500
D SIZE_OF_DS      C                   CONST(%SIZE(MULTOCCDS:*ALL))
D NUM             S               5P 0

 * NUM will equal 5
C                   EVAL      NUM = %SIZE(-005.00)

 * NUM will equal 5
C                   EVAL      NUM = %SIZE(005.00)

 * NUM will equal 7
C                   EVAL      NUM = %SIZE('ILE RPG')

 * NUM will equal 11
C                   EVAL      NUM = %SIZE('   ILE RPG   ')

 * NUM will equal 7
C                   EVAL      NUM = %SIZE(PACKNUM)

 * NUM will equal 4
C                   EVAL      NUM = %SIZE(BINNUM)

 * NUM will equal 15
C                   EVAL      NUM = %SIZE(SIGNNUM)

 * NUM will equal 40
C                   EVAL      NUM = %SIZE(CHARVAR)

 * NUM will equal 3
C                   EVAL      NUM = %SIZE(PACKARR)

 * NUM will equal 30
C                   EVAL      NUM = %SIZE(PACKARR:*ALL)
```

```
 * NUM will equal 5
C                     EVAL      NUM = %SIZE(SIGNARR)

 * NUM will equal 50
C                     EVAL      NUM = %SIZE(SIGNARR:*ALL)

 * NUM will equal 11
C                     EVAL      NUM = %SIZE(CHARARR)

 * NUM will equal 55
C                     EVAL      NUM = %SIZE(CHARARR:*ALL)

 * NUM will equal 8
C                     EVAL      NUM = %SIZE(MULTOCCDS)

 * NUM will equal 160
C                     EVAL      NUM = %SIZE(MULTOCCDS:*ALL)

 * NUM will equal 8
C                     EVAL      NUM = %SIZE(CHARCON)

 * NUM will equal 3
C                     EVAL      NUM = %SIZE(NUMCON)
```

SUMMARY

Built-in functions can substantially reduce program development and maintenance time. In some cases, complex routines or called programs in RPG/400 are reduced to a single line of code in ILE RPG.

Chapter 11

Date and Time Data Types

Date, time, and time-stamp data types were introduced to the OS/400 database in V2R1M1. Unfortunately, RPG/400 didn't support these useful data types. The RPG programmer was always faced with the tediousness of manipulating dates as normal character or numeric fields. As a result, there are probably as many date handling routines written in RPG as there are RPG programmers.

The good news is ILE RPG supports date, time, and time-stamp data types. This means you can add or subtract dates to and from each other, and you can add or subtract durations to and from dates. In other words, you can perform date arithmetic.

This support makes it easy to calculate the difference between two dates or to increment a date by a number of days, taking into account the varying number of days in each month. For example, 1992 is a leap year. If you add 30 days to January 31, 1992, ILE RPG correctly calculates the result as March 1, 1992; if you add 30 days to January 31, 1993, the result is March 2, 1993.

You are also able to perform similar types of calculations with time and time-stamp data. ILE RPG provides support for conversion from one date type to another, and conversion to and from numeric and character fields. So, even if you don't convert your old character and numeric date and time fields in your database, you'll at least be able to convert them internally to the new date data type so you can take advantage of the date functions. With ILE RPG, date manipulation has forever changed for the better.

DATE, TIME, AND TIME-STAMP DATA TYPES

DDS has supported date, time, and time-stamp data types for some time. Because these data types are not directly supported in RPG/400, they have been of little practical use for RPG programmers. ILE RPG is about to change that.

Table 11.1 shows the eight date formats currently supported for date fields. The date format controls the order and length of the month, day, and year. In addition, the date format specifies the default separator character of forward slash, hyphen, or period. The year can be represented in 2-byte (YY) and 4-byte (YYYY) character format. The Day of the month (DD) is represented in 2-byte format, while the Julian Day (DDD) is represented in 3-byte format. The Month (MM) is always represented in 2-byte format.

Table 11.1: Date Data Types

Date Format Parameter	Description	Date Format and Separator	Presentation Length (bytes)	Internal Length (bytes)	Example
*MDY	Month/Day/Year	MM/DD/YY	8	4	12/16/94
*DMY	Day/Month/Year	DD/MM/YY	8	4	16/12/94
*YMD	Year/Month/Day	YY/MM/DD	8	4	94/12/16
*JUL	Julian	YY/DDD	6	4	94/350
*ISO	International Standards Organization	YYYY-MM-DD	10	4	1994-12-16
*USA	IBM USA Standard	MM/DD/YYYY	10	4	12/16/1994
*EUR	IBM European Standard	DD.MM.YYYY	10	4	16.12.1994
*JIS	Japanese Industrial Standard	YYYY-MM-DD	10	4	1994-12-16

The internal length is the number of bytes of storage required to store the date field on disk without the separator characters. All date fields, regardless of date format, require 4 bytes of storage. The presentation length is the number of bytes of storage required to represent the date in a program, on a screen, or in a report, including the separator characters. Date fields require between 6 and 10 characters of storage for presentation, depending upon the date format specified. Leading zeros are required for all date formats except *USA.

ILE RPG supports five time formats, as shown in Table 11.2. The time format designates whether or not 12- or 24-hour format is used and seconds are shown. In addition, the time format specifies the default separator character of colon or period. Hours (HH) and Minutes (MM) are represented in 2-byte format. Seconds (ss) are represented in 2-byte format for 24-hour time, or AM or PM is represented in 2-byte format for 12-hour time.

Table 11.2: Time Data Types

Time Format Parameter	Description	Time Format and Separator	Presentation Length (bytes)	Internal Length (bytes)	Example
*HMS	Hours:Minutes:Seconds	HH:MM:SS	8	3	18:06:30
*ISO	International Standards Organization	HH.MM.SS	8	3	18.06.30
*USA	IBM USA Standard	HH:MM AM or HH:MM PM	8	3	6:06 PM
*EUR	IBM European Standard	HH.MM.SS	8	3	18.06.30
*JIS	Japanese Industrial Standard	HH:MM:SS	8	3	18:06:30

The internal length of a time field is always 3 bytes. Time fields always require 8 bytes for presentation regardless of the time format specified. Leading zeros are required for all time formats except *USA.

Fields with a time-stamp data type always have the same format as shown in Table 11.3. Year (YYYY) is always 4 bytes and is followed by Month (MM), Day (DD), Hours (HH), Minutes (MM), and Seconds (SS), which are always 2 bytes. Microseconds (UUUUUU) is last with 6 bytes. The separator characters are always a combination of hyphens for the date and periods for the time.

Table 11.3: Time-stamp Data Types

Format	Presentation Length (bytes)	Internal Length (bytes)	Example
YYYY-MM-DD-HH.MM.SS.UUUUUU	26	10	1994-12-16-18.06.30.000001

The internal length of a time-stamp field is always 10 bytes. Time-stamp fields always require 26 bytes for presentation. If microseconds are not specified when a time-stamp value is used in ILE RPG, the compiler pads the value with zeros.

Within ILE RPG, you can define fields or constants as date (D), time (T), or time-stamp (Z) data types. For the rest of this chapter, such fields are referred to generically as date fields unless an example specifically applies to time or time-stamp fields. The length of a date field is determined by the data type and the date format—it should not be coded as part of the definition.

The default format for date fields in an ILE RPG program can be specified in the H-spec using the DATFMT and TIMFMT keywords. (For more information on H-spec keywords, see Chapter 4.) If these keywords are not used, the default format is International Standards Organization (*ISO) format (see Table 11.1).

DATE FIELD DEFINITIONS

Figure 11.1 shows examples of defining date and time fields with initialized values. No H-spec exists in the program, so date fields that do not include a DATFMT or TIMFMT keyword default to *ISO format.

In the first example in Figure 11.1, the D in position 40 (Internal Data Type) defines the field eur_date as a date field. *EUR is specified for the DATFMT keyword, so the date is internally represented in IBM European Standard format (that is, DD.MM.YYYY) and is automatically defined as 10 characters in length. The INZ parameter initializes the field to a value of 16.12.1994 (December 16, 1994).

Figure 11.1: Defining Date/Time Fields Initialized in Default *ISO Format

```
*. 1 ...+... 2 ...+... 3 ...+... 4 ...+... 5 ...+... 6 ...+... 7 ...+... 8 ...+... 9 ...+... 10
HFunctions+++++++++++++++++++++++++++++++++++++++++++++++++++++++++++++++++++Comments++++++++++++
H
DName++++++++++ETDsFrom+++To/L+++IDc.Functions..........................Comments++++++++++++
D eur_date        S              D    DATFMT(*EUR) INZ(D'1994-12-16')     16.12.1994
D usa_date        S              D    DATFMT(*USA) INZ(D'1994-12-16')     12/16/1994
D iso_date        S              D    INZ(D'1994-12-16')                  1994-12-16

D hms_time        S              T    TIMFMT(*HMS) INZ(T'18.06.30')       18:06:30
D usa_time        S              T    TIMFMT(*USA) INZ(T'18.06.30')       6:06  PM
D iso_time        S              T    INZ(T'18.06.30')                    18.06.30
```

Even though the field eur_date is defined as a *EUR format date field, the value on the INZ parameter must be in *ISO format (that is, 1994-12-16). This is because literals can not be specified for a date field format that is different from the default date and time format of the program. The value for all date and time literals must be represented in the format specified in the H-spec, or *ISO format if no format is specified.

Several other examples of date field definitions are included in Figure 11.1. The T in position 40 defines the field hms_time as a time field. Because *HMS is specified for the TIMFMT keyword, the time is internally represented in the Hours:Minutes:Seconds format (that is, HH.MM.SS). The INZ parameter initializes the field to 30 seconds after 6:06 p.m. In a similar manner, the field usa_time is defined as a *USA format time field with an implied length of eight. While the internal format of this field is HH:MM AM or HH:MM PM, the value on the INZ parameter must be in *ISO format (that is, HH.MM.SS).

Prefix date literals with D, T, and Z for date, time, and time-stamp values. Using the *ISO format, D'1994-12-16' defines a date literal with a length of 10 and a value of December 16, 1994. T'18.06.30' defines a time literal with a length of eight and a value of 30 seconds after 6:06 p.m. Z'1994-12-16-18.06.30' defines a time-stamp literal with a length of 26 and a value of 30 seconds after 6:06 p.m. on December 16, 1994. (If the microseconds portion of a time-stamp literal is not specified, it defaults to '000000' and its length remains 26).

Figure 11.2 shows another sample of defining date and time fields with initialized values. In this sample, a DATFMT of *USA and TIMFMT of *HMS are specified on the H-spec.

Figure 11.2: Defining Date/Time Fields Initialized in *USA and *HMS Formats

```
*. 1 ...+... 2 ...+... 3 ...+... 4 ...+... 5 ...+... 6 ...+... 7 ...+... 8 ...+... 9 ...+... 10
HFunctions++++++++++++++++++++++++++++++++++++++++++++++++++++++++++++++++++++Comments+++++++++++
H DATFMT(*USA) TIMFMT(*HMS)


DName++++++++++ETDsFrom+++To/L+++IDc.Functions...........................Comments+++++++++++
D eur_date        S              D   DATFMT(*EUR) INZ(D'12/16/1994')      16.12.1994
D eur_date2       S                  LIKE(eur_date) INZ(D'05/18/1995')    18.05.1995
D usa_date        S              D   INZ(D'12/16/1994')                   12/16/1994
D iso_date        S              D   DATFMT(*ISO) INZ(D'12/16/1994')      1994-12-16

D usa_time        S              T   TIMFMT(*USA) INZ(T'18:06:30')        6:06 PM
D hms_time        S              T   INZ(T'18:06:30')                     18:06:30
D iso_time        S              T   TIMFMT(*ISO) INZ(T'18:06:30')        18.06.30
```

As in the prior example, the field eur_date is defined as a 10-character, *EUR-format (DD.MM.YYYY) date field. But this time, the initialization value must be provided in *USA format (MM/DD/YYYY) because of the *USA value specified in the DATFMT keyword in the H-spec.

When the LIKE keyword is used, the DATFMT and TIMFMT keywords are not allowed. The field eur_date2 is defined as a 10-character, *EUR-format (DD.MM.YYYY) date field that takes its format (but not its value) from the field eur_date.

The value of the field usa_date is 12/16/1994. As with the *EUR format, the iso_date field initialization value must be provided in *USA format (MM/DD/YYYY).

DEFAULT VALUES

The previous material showed how date fields can be initialized to a specific value using the INZ keyword in the D-specs. You can also initialize a date field using the CLEAR operation code in the C-specs. The default initialization and CLEAR value is not all zeros, as might be expected. For date fields, the default value is January 1, 0001; for time fields, the default value is midnight; and for time-stamp fields, the default value is midnight on January 1, 0001. In all cases, the format includes separator characters and is based on the DATFMT and TIMFMT parameters or the default *ISO format. If the DATFMT and TIMFMT keywords are not specified in either the H-spec or the D-spec, the cleared value of a date field is 0001-01-01, the cleared value of a time field is 00.00.00, and the cleared value of a time-stamp field is 0001-01-01-00.00.00.000000. The value set by *LOVAL is the same as the CLEAR value.

The value set by *HIVAL is December 31, 9999, for a date field; 1 second before midnight (23.59.59) for a time field; and 1 microsecond before midnight on December 31, 9999, for a time-stamp field (9999-12-31-23.59.59.999999).

COMPARING DATE FIELDS

Date data types can be used in factor 1 and factor 2 for many ILE RPG operation codes. As with other types of fields, you can compare date fields only if they have the same data type—date, time, or time stamp. ILE RPG automatically handles different formats—an *ISO-format time field with a value of 15.30.00 compares equally to a *USA-format time field with a value of 03:30 PM. In the same way, a *MDY-format date field with a value of 12/16/94 compares equally to a *YMD-format date field with a value of 94/12/16.

DATE ARITHMETIC

Arithmetic operations are where the new date data types really shine. Many RPG/400 programs use a complex subroutine that accounts for leap years and the varying number of days in each month to calculate the difference between two dates or to increment a date by a specific number of days. You can get the same results with much less effort using date fields and several new operation codes.

The Add Duration (ADDDUR) operation code can be used to add a duration to a date, time, or time-stamp field, resulting in a field of the same type. Factor 1 is optional and, if not specified, defaults to the result field. Factor 1 and the result field must be the same data type.

Factor 2 is required and contains two parts separated by a colon. The first part must be a numeric field, array element, or constant with zero decimal positions; it represents the duration to be added. The second part is a code indicating the type of duration. The duration code must be valid for the data type of the field specified in the result field. For example, you can not add a minute duration to a date type field. The valid duration codes are *YEARS or *Y, *MONTHS or *M, *DAYS or *D, *HOURS or *H, *MINUTES or *MN, *SECONDS or *S, and *MSECONDS or *MS.

An error indicator can be specified in positions 73 and 74. If an error occurs, the result field remains unchanged and the error indicator, if specified, is set on. An error occurs in any of the following situations:

♦   The date, time, or time-stamp field in factor 1 contains invalid data.

♦   Factor 1 is not specified and the date, time, or time-stamp field in the result field contains invalid data.

♦   The result of the operation is invalid.

Figure 11.3 shows some examples of using the ADDDUR operation code. No H-spec is present, so all date and time values are specified in *ISO format.

Figure 11.3: Examples of the ADDDUR Operation

```
    *. 1 ...+... 2 ...+... 3 ...+... 4 ...+... 5 ...+... 6 ...+... 7 ...+... 8
    DName++++++++++ETDsFrom+++To/L+++IDc.Functions..........................
    D start_date      S             D   DATFMT(*ISO) INZ(D'1994-12-16')
    D end_date        S             D   DATFMT(*ISO)
    D month_end       S             D   DATFMT(*USA) INZ(D'1994-10-31')
    D employ_dat      S             D   DATFMT(*USA) INZ(D'1992-02-29')
    D anniv_dat       S             D   DATFMT(*USA)
    D end_time        S             T   TIMFMT(*HMS)
    D total_time      S             Z


    CL0N01Factor1+++++++Opcode(E)+Factor2+++++++Result+++++++Len++D+HiLoEq....
     * Add 30 days to date
     *
    C     start_date    adddur    30:*days      end_date              50
     *
     * Add 1 month to date
     *
    C                   adddur    1:*months     month_end
     *
     * Add 1 year to date
     *
    C     employ_dat    adddur    1:*years      anniv_dat
     *
     * Add 3 hours, 22 minutes and 50 seconds to midnight
     *
```

```
C       T'00.00.00'   adddur     3:*hours       end_time
C                     adddur    22:*mn          end_time
C                     adddur    50:*seconds     end_time
 *
 * Add 1000 microseconds to a timestamp
 *
C                     adddur  1000:*ms          total_time
```

The first C-spec adds 30 days to the field start_date and stores the result in the field end_date. Both start_date and end_date are defined as date fields with an *ISO format and an implied length of 10. The field start_date is initialized to 1994-12-16, so the field end_date has a value of 1995-01-15 after execution of the ADDDUR operation code. If an error occurs, indicator 50 is turned on. Indicator 50 is turned off if no error occurs.

In the second example in Figure 11.3, one month is being added to the *USA format date field month_end. The field month_end is initialized to a value of 10/31/1994 in D-specs. Adding one month to the month portion of this date would result in an invalid date of 11/31/1994; but the result of the ADDDUR operation is automatically adjusted to the last valid day of the month. The field month_end has the value 11/30/1994 after execution of the ADDDUR operation code.

In the next example, one year is added to the field employ_dat and the result is stored in the field anniv_dat. The field employ_dat is initialized to a value of 02/29/1992 in D-specs. Adding one year to this date without any adjustment would result in an invalid date of 02/29/1993; 1993 is not a leap year. But the result of the ADDDUR operation is automatically adjusted to the last valid day of the month. The field anniv_dat has the value 02/28/1993 after execution of the ADDDUR operation code.

The next example demonstrates the use of the ADDDUR operation code with time fields. The first calculation adds three hours to the literal in factor 1, which is set to midnight. The time constant is expressed in *ISO format, using a period as a separator character, even though the result field end_time is defined in *HMS format using a colon as a separator character. The next two lines of code add 22 minutes and 50 seconds to end_time, giving a result of 03:22:50.

The Subtract Duration (SUBDUR) operation code follows the same rules as ADDDUR to subtract durations from date fields. The result field is required and must be the same data type as factor 1 if factor 1 is specified. Several examples are shown in Figure 11.4.

Figure 11.4: Examples of the SUBDUR Operation

```
 *.  1 ...+... 2 ...+... 3 ...+... 4 ...+... 5 ...+... 6 ...+... 7 ...+... 8
HFunctions+++++++++++++++++++++++++++++++++++++++++++++++++++++++++++++++++++++
H DATFMT(*USA) TIMFMT(*HMS)

DName+++++++++++ETDsFrom+++To/L+++IDc.Functions..........................
D start_date      S               D    DATFMT(*ISO)
D end_date        S               D    DATFMT(*ISO) INZ(D'01/04/1995')
D month_end       S               D    DATFMT(*USA) INZ(D'10/31/1994')
D employ_dat      S               D    DATFMT(*USA)
D anniv_dat       S               D    DATFMT(*USA) INZ(D'02/29/1992')
D start_time      S               Z    INZ(Z'1994-05-12-02.59.40')
D end_time        S               Z    INZ(Z'1994-05-12-03.22.50')
D loan_date       S               D    INZ(D'12/16/1993')
D due_date        S               D    INZ(D'12/16/2008')

CL0N01Factor1++++++++Opcode(E)+Factor2+++++++Result++++++++Len++D+HiLoEq....
 *
 * Subtract 30 days from date
 *
C     end_date       subdur    30:*days       start_date           50
 *
 * Subtract 1 month from date
 *
C                    subdur    1:*months      month_end
 *
 * Subtract 1 year from date
 *
C     anniv_date     subdur    1:*years       employ_dat
 *
 * Calculate number of seconds between start and stop timestamps
 *
C     end_time       subdur    start_time     num_sec:*secs       7 0
 *
 * Calculate number of days between dates
 *
C     due_date       subdur    loan_date      num_mon:*m          3 0
CL0N01Factor1++++++++Opcode(E)+Factor2+++++++Result++++++++Len++D+HiLoEq....
```

The SUBDUR operation can also be used to calculate the duration (or difference) between:

- Two date fields.

- A date and a time-stamp field.

- Two time fields.

♦ A time and a time-stamp field.

♦ Two time-stamp fields.

When calculating a duration, both factor 1 and factor 2 must be specified and must be compatible types as specified above. A date and a time stamp are compatible as are a time and a time stamp. ILE RPG handles any conversion between date or time formats (that is, a *USA date subtracted from an *ISO date).

The result field is also required and contains two parts. The first must be a numeric field, an array element, or a constant with zero decimal positions in which the result is placed. The second is separated from the first by a colon and must be a valid duration code indicating the type of duration. The result is negative if the date or time in factor 1 is earlier than the date or time in factor 2.

Figure 11.4 shows some examples of using the SUBDUR operation code. DATFMT(*USA) is specified on the H-spec, so all date literals must be provided in *USA format. Because TIMFMT(*HMS) is also specified, all time literals must be provided in *HMS format.

The first three examples are very similar to the examples for ADDDUR in the previous section. A duration is subtracted from a date, resulting in a new date. If necessary, ILE RPG automatically adjusts the result to a valid date, taking into account leap year and the number of days in each month.

The fourth example demonstrates the use of the SUBDUR operation code with time-stamp fields to determine the difference between two time-stamp values. The field start_time is defined as a time-stamp field with a value of 1994-05-12- 02.59.40, and the field end_time is defined as a time-stamp field with a value of 1994-05-12-03.22.50. Microseconds default to all zeros. The duration code *SECS is specified on the result field, so the field num_sec has a value of 1,390 seconds after execution of the SUBDUR operation code.

In the last example, the date field loan_date, which has a value of 12/16/1993, is subtracted from the date field due_date, which has a value of 12/16/2008. The duration code *M (Months) is specified on the result field, so the field num_mon has a value of 180 months.

EXTRCT Operation Code

The Extract (EXTRCT) operation code can be used to extract a portion of a date field. Factor 1 must be blank. Factor 2 is required and contains two parts separated by a colon. The first part must be a date, time, or time-stamp field. The second part must be a duration code that is valid for the data type of the field specified in the first part of factor 2. For example, you can extract hours from a time or time-stamp field but not from a date field.

The result field may be a numeric or character field. Before the EXTRCT operation is executed, the result field is cleared. Numeric result fields are right-justified while character result fields are left-justified.

The first three examples in Figure 11.5 extract information from the field due_date, which is defined as an *ISO format date field and initialized to 2008-12-16. The month is extracted into the character field char_month with a result of 12. The day is extracted into the character field char_day with a result of 16. The year is extracted into the numeric field num_year with a result of 1994.

Figure 11.5: Examples of the EXTRCT Operation

```
*. 1 ...+... 2 ...+... 3 ...+... 4 ...+... 5 ...+... 6 ...+... 7 ...+... 8
DName+++++++++++ETDsFrom+++To/L+++IDc.Functions...........................
D due_date        S             D   INZ(D'2008-12-16')
D start_time      S             Z   INZ(Z'1994-10-22-02.59.40')

CL0N01Factor1+++++++Opcode(E)+Factor2+++++++Result++++++++Len++D+HiLoEq....
 *
 * Extract month, day and year
 *
C                   extrct    due_date:*m   char_month       2
C                   extrct    due_date:*d   char_day         2
C                   extrct    due_date:*y   num_year         4 0
 *
 * Extract month and hours
 *
C                   extrct    start_time:*m char_month
C                   extrct    start_time:*h num_hour         2 0
```

The second group of examples uses the field start_time, which is defined as a time-stamp field and initialized to a value of 1994-10-22-02.59.40. The month is extracted into the character field char_month with a result of 10, and the hour is extracted into the numeric field num_hour with a result of 2.

CONVERTING DATE FORMATS

The MOVE and MOVEL operation codes can be used to convert date, time, and time-stamp fields from one data type or format to another. The valid conversions are:

♦ Date to date, time stamp, character, or numeric.

♦ Time to time, time stamp, character, or numeric.

♦ Time stamp to date, time, character, or numeric.

♦ Character or numeric to date, time, or time stamp.

You can use the Move Array (MOVEA) operation code only to move date data type fields to a character type field, array, or array element. As with any move operation, when you use one of the MOVE operation codes to convert from one data type to another, the value in factor 2 is moved to the result field.

Factor 1 is optional and is used to specify the format of factor 2 when factor 2 is not a date data type. Alternatively, factor 1 can be used to specify the format of the result field when the result field is not a date data type. All of the date formats are valid and, in addition, *JOBRUN can be used to indicate that the date format values from the job should be used. If factor 1 is not specified, then the DATFMT and TIMFMT values in the H-spec are used if specified; otherwise, *ISO format is assumed. Factor 1 must be blank if both factor 2 and the result field are date data types. In this case, ILE RPG automatically converts from one date format to another.

When a MOVE operation code is used to convert a character field to a date type field, the character field must include the separators required by the format specified in factor 1. Conversely, when a date field is moved to a character field, the character field contains separators based upon the format specified in factor 1. Separators are not permitted when moving a numeric field to a date field, nor are they inserted when moving a date field to a numeric field.

Figure 11.6 shows some examples of converting dates using the MOVE operation code. In the first example, the field start_num is defined as a zoned decimal field in which we are storing a date in YYMMDD format (941216). We want to add 30 days to the value in start_num. In RPG/400, this requires a subroutine that accounts for leap years and the number of days in each month; but, as Figure 11.6 illustrates, it is a simple process in ILE RPG.

Figure 11.6: Converting Dates Using the MOVE Operation

```
*. 1 ...+... 2 ...+... 3 ...+... 4 ...+... 5 ...+... 6 ...+... 7 ...+... 8...+... 9 ...+... 10
* No H-spec so dates and times default to *ISO format.


DName++++++++++ETDsFrom+++To/L+++IDc.Functions...........................Comments+++++++++++
D start_num       S             6S 0 INZ(941216)
D start_date      S                D    DATFMT(*ISO)
D usa_date        S                D    DATFMT(*USA)  INZ(D'1916-04-16')
04/16/1916
D eur_date        S                D    DATFMT(*EUR)
D ymd_date        S                D    DATFMT(*YMD)


CL0N01Factor1++++++++Opcode(E)+Factor2+++++++Result+++++++Len++D+HiLoEq....Comments+++++++++++
 *
 * Add 30 days to date stored as a number in YYMMDD format
 *
C     *YMD          move      start_num      start_date        start_date=1994-12-16
C                   adddur    30:*days       start_date        start_date=1995-01-15
C     *YMD          move      start_date     start_num         start_num=950115
 *
 * Convert a date from *USA to *EUR format
 *
C                   move      usa_date       eur_date          eur_date=16.04.1916
 *
 * Cannot convert a date before 1940 or after 2039 to *YMD format
 *
C                   move      usa_date       ymd_date          run time error
```

First, use the MOVE operation code to convert the zoned decimal field start_num to the *ISO date start_date. Factor 1 indicates the field start_num is in *YMD format (for example, YYMMDD). Then all we have to do is use the ADDDUR operation code to add 30 days to start_date and MOVE the *ISO date field start_date back to the zoned decimal field start_num. Again, factor 1 indicates the field start_num is to be formatted in *YMD format. The field start_num has the value 950115.

In the next example, the move operation code is used to convert a date from *USA to *EUR format. The field usa_date is defined as a *USA-format field with a value of 04/16/1916. The field eur_date is defined as a *EUR-format field. Moving the field usa_date to the field eur_date results in eur_date having the value 16.04.1916.

The final example demonstrates a potential problem for those who store their dates in MMDDYY, DDMMYY, or YYMMDD format. Dates in these formats must be in the range of 1940 to 2039. Attempting to move a value outside of this range to this format date results in a run-time error. The *USA-format date usa_date has a value of 04/16/1916, which is before 1940, so attempting to move this date to the *YMD-format date ymd_date causes a run-time error.

Many people store their dates in packed decimal fields in CYYMMDD format where C represents the century (for example, 0941216 represents 12/16/1994 and 1941216 represents 12/16/2094). *CYMD is not currently supported as a convert-from or convert-to date format.

SUMMARY

It's been a long time coming, but real date support has finally made it to RPG. Date manipulation for RPG programmers no longer needs to be the dreaded chore it was for so many years.

With the ADDDUR operation, you can add a duration to a date or time. With the SUBDUR operation, you can subtract a duration from a date or time, or calculate the duration between two dates, times, or time stamps. With EXTRCT (Extract Date/Time/Time Stamp), you can test for a valid date, time, or time-stamp field.

Chapter 12

Debugging ILE Programs

When it comes to tracking down a problem in your program, tracing the actual program code while the program is running is the quickest method for finding the problem. This method, known as *source-level debugging*, has been around for years.

Unfortunately for AS/400 programmers, source-level debugging wasn't available from IBM until recently. Unless you were willing to purchase a third-party source debugger, you were faced with using the very limited OS/400 system debugger, which required that you have the most recent source listing of a program before you could use it effectively. Even then, it was cumbersome. The good news is that, with V3R1, IBM gives you a source-level debug function for ILE languages, including RPG.

With a source-level debugger, the program source statements are displayed on your workstation as the program is running. By stopping at selected statements (setting breakpoints), you can control how much of your program runs before you examine it by displaying the values of the program variables.

When the program reaches a breakpoint, the program stops. The debugger displays the statement to which the breakpoint has been assigned and the statements surrounding it. You can easily examine and change the variables used in that particular section of code. Of course, you can also page through other sections of the source, trace through source code a single line at a time, or examine any variable defined in your program.

Introducing ILE Source Debugger

All of the ILE languages on the AS/400 use the new system debugger, which provides an interface that can display program source statements during a debug session. A debug session can be established for an interactive program, or for a batch program for which you have run the Start Service Job (STRSRVJOB) command. The new system debugger, known as the ILE source debugger, offers these options:

- View the program source.

- Set and remove conditional and unconditional breakpoints.

- Step through a specified number of statements.

- Display or change the value of fields, structures, and arrays.

- Equate shorthand names for fields, expressions, or debug commands.

The source-level debug functions of the system debugger are only available to ILE programs. However, you can perform source-level debugging for Original Program Model (OPM) RPG, COBOL, and CL programs with the Interactive Source Debugger (ISDB). ISDB is a free component of the Application Development ToolSet/400 (ADTS/400) beginning with V3R1. For more information about ISDB, see the IBM *Interactive Source Debugger* manual, document number SC09-1897.

Some ILE Review

Before you can understand the ILE source debugger, you need to know a little about ILE. ILE concepts were covered in Chapter 2. If you haven't read that chapter, or would like a brief review, the following material will help you understand the ILE source debugger.

The notion of modularity in programming has been around for some time. Ideally, an application is made up of small, single-purpose programs that call each other when a certain function is required. Of course, smaller programs mean more programs and more programs calling other programs (external program calls).

Before ILE, external program calls could only be performed one way—dynamically. Resolution of dynamic calls (the link between one program and another separately compiled program) occur at run time and require significant system overhead. Therefore, on the AS/400, a programmer could only break programs down so much before the performance of the application would degrade beyond a tolerable level. This is one reason most AS/400 programs tend to be large.

With ILE, you can get around the performance issue of dynamic calls by linking your programs together as if they were one program. ILE languages use an intermediate object that is created from program source code. This intermediate object is known as a module object (object type *MODULE) and is not executable. One or more modules are linked together to create the program object (object type *PGM). Any module, no matter what language is used to create it, can be linked to another module. Combining modules into a single executable program is called binding.

Modules within a program can be called by one another just like programs call each other. Calls to modules are known as bound calls. The ILE RPG operation for a bound call is CALLB. The difference between a bound call and a dynamic call is that having modules call one another within a program is much faster than performing external program calls dynamically at run time. Essentially, an ILE programmer can break an application into smaller, simpler, and more maintainable pieces without concern about performance degradation. For more information on ILE, see the IBM *AS/400 Integrated Language Environment Concepts* manual.

Now that you understand a little about modules, you can better understand the ILE debugger.

BEFORE YOU DEBUG

Before you can debug an ILE program at the source level, you must create the modules with the Debug view (DBGVIEW) parameter set to a value that gives you the view you want. The three views available are Statement, Root (source), and List.

♦ The Statement view displays no source statements and is the default debug view for the Create Program (CRTPGM) command and the Create xxx Module (CRTxxxMOD) command (xxx is the language abbreviation). Change the view to Root or List when you create your ILE modules or programs, or you won't be able to perform any source-level debugging.

♦ The Root view displays the source statements found in the module source member.

♦ The List view displays the source statements generated on the compile listing. Normally, these include any source member statements, any statements included from externally described files, and any source statements included by the /COPY compiler directive.

USING THE DEBUGGER

With the ILE source debugger, you actually debug at the module level—not the program level. Unlike OPM programs, which store observability information in the program, ILE programs store observability in the program modules. ILE observability is now split into two parts—debug information and the program template. Figure 12.1 illustrates how ILE observability is stored.

Figure 12.1: Observability Information and ILE Programs

ILE Program

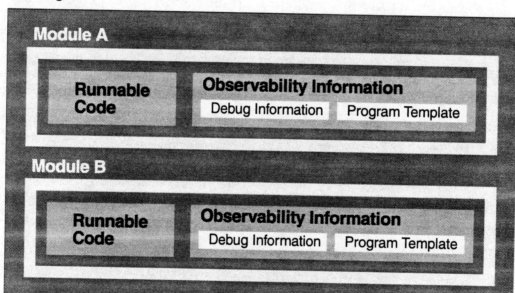

To start the source debugger, the same Start Debug (STRDBG) command is used. The system determines whether the program you want to debug is an OPM or an ILE program. If it's an OPM program, the debugger works the same as before, and you can use the traditional debug commands, such as Add Breakpoint (ADDBKP) and

Add Trace (ADDTRC). If the program is an ILE program and you created the modules with the appropriate debug view, you are presented with the Display Module Source display (Figure 12.2).

Figure 12.2: The Display Module Source Display

```
                        Display Module Source

Program:   DBGEX03RG       Library:    ILERPG        Module:   DBGEX03RG
    1         DCHRSTR06         S              7A   INZ('MoJoMan')
    2
    3         DPKDDEC0502       S              5P 2 INZ(125.30)
    4
    5         DBINARY0902       S              9B 2 INZ(1234567.89)
    6
    7         DARRAY            S              3S 2 DIM(2) INZ(1.25)
    8
    9         DYYMMDD           DS
   10         D YY                            2A   INZ('94')
   11         D MM                            2A   INZ('12')
   12         D DD                            2A   INZ('25')
   13
   14         C                 EVAL       *INLR = *ON

                                                                  Bottom

Debug . . . _____

 F3=End program    F6=Add/Clear breakpoint   F10=Step   F11=Display variable
 F12=Resume        F13=Work with module breakpoints     F24=More keys
```

This initial display allows you to set breakpoints. Unfortunately, you can't start the program from the initial display; you must get to a command line to start it. If you defined any breakpoints, the Display Module Source screen reappears when a breakpoint is reached, and the source code is positioned at the breakpoint that was taken.

You do most of your debugging from the Display Module Source screen. As shown in Figure 12.2, there is a command line at the bottom of the display. This is a debug command line where you can enter special debug commands. For example, you can enter the Attributes (ATTR) command to display the attributes of a variable, the Breakpoint (BREAK) command to set an unconditional or a conditional breakpoint, or the Evaluate (EVAL) command to display the value of a variable. You can also use the HELP command to display a list of valid commands with brief descriptions. Table 12.1 contains a complete list of the ILE debugger commands, the command abbreviations, and a summarized description.

Table 12.1: The ILE Source Debugger Commands

Command	Abbreviation	Description
ATTR	A	Displays the attributes of a variable (type and length).
BREAK	BR	Enters unconditional and conditional breakpoints.
CLEAR	C	Removes unconditional and conditional breakpoints.
DISPLAY	DI	Displays the names and definitions assigned by using the EQUATE command. Also allows you to display a different source module.
EQUATE	EQ	Assigns an expression, variable, or debug command to a name for shorthand use.
EVAL	EV	Displays or changes the value of a variable, or displays the value of expressions, records, structures, or arrays.
QUAL	Q	Defines the scope of variables that appear in subsequent EVAL commands. Does not apply to ILE RPG.
STEP	S	Runs one or more statements of the program being debugged.
FIND	F	Searches forward or backward in the module currently displayed for a specified line number, string, or text.
UP	U	Moves the displayed window of source toward the beginning of the view by the amount entered.
DOWN	DO	Moves the displayed window of source toward the end of the view by the amount entered.
LEFT	L	Moves the displayed window of source to the left by the amount entered.
RIGHT	R	Moves the displayed window of source to the right by the amount entered.
TOP	T	Positions the view to show the first line.

Command	Abbreviation	Description
BOTTOM	BO	Positions the view to show the last line.
NEXT	N	Positions the view to the next breakpoint in the source currently displayed.
PREVIOUS	P	Positions the view to the previous breakpoint in the source currently displayed.
HELP	H	Shows the online help information for the available source debugger commands.

Suppose you want to examine some variables in the program being debugged in Figure 12.2. First, establish a breakpoint so the program stops running before it completes. Place the cursor on the last (only) C-spec and press the Toggle Breakpoint function key (F6). A message displays at the bottom of the screen, "Breakpoint added to line 14." Exit the Display Module Source display with F3 or F12, and then call the program. The program runs until the breakpoint is reached. Then the program source displays again. Now you can examine any of the program fields.

Say you want to examine the PKDDEC0502 field. Either position the cursor in the field and press F11, or use the EVAL debug command at the command line:

```
EVAL PKDDEC0502
```

The field value is displayed at the bottom of the screen as PKDDEC0502 = 125.30.

To display the hexadecimal value of field PKDFLD0502, you must use the EVAL command (you can't use the F11 key), with a slight modification. Key in this command:

```
EVAL PKDFLD0502: X
```

to display the hexadecimal value at the bottom of the screen. If you want to display the hexadecimal value of the BINARY0902 field (you still can not use the F11 key), use the EVAL command syntax just as you did for the PKDFLD0502 field:

```
EVAL BINARY0902: X
```

The hexadecimal value of BINARY0902 appears at the bottom of the screen. To display the value of the YYMMDD data structure, position the cursor in the YYMMDD data structure name and use the F11 key or the EVAL command:

```
EVAL YYMMDD
```

This time, the Evaluate Expression display appears, as illustrated in Figure 12.3. Notice that the screen displays all subfield values for data structure YYMMDD. Similarly, if you display an array, the debugger displays all elements of the array. The Evaluate Expression display appears because the value of the data structure YYMMDD can not be displayed at the bottom of the screen on a single line.

Figure 12.3: The Evaluate Expression Display

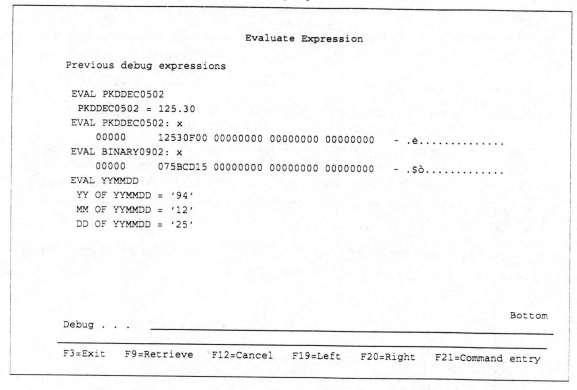

```
                              Evaluate Expression

     Previous debug expressions


     EVAL PKDDEC0502
      PKDDEC0502 = 125.30
     EVAL PKDDEC0502: x
         00000     12530F00 00000000 00000000 00000000   - .ë.............
     EVAL BINARY0902: x
         00000     075BCD15 00000000 00000000 00000000   - .sò.............
     EVAL YYMMDD
      YY OF YYMMDD = '94'
      MM OF YYMMDD = '12'
      DD OF YYMMDD = '25'




                                                                    Bottom
     Debug . . .   _____


     F3=Exit    F9=Retrieve   F12=Cancel   F19=Left   F20=Right   F21=Command entry
```

You can also display the Evaluate Expression screen by pressing Enter from the Display Module Source screen when the command line is empty. The Evaluate Expression display is useful if you are displaying a number of variables and you need to review what you have seen.

A powerful optional feature of the EVAL command is its ability to change a program variable. For example, to change the value of field CHRSTR06 from MoJoMan to MoJoBoy, key in this command:

```
EVAL CHRSTR06 = 'MoJoBoy'
```

You can assign a value to a character variable using a hexadecimal value by qualifying the character literal with an X. For example, say you want to assign the logical not character () to a variable called SYMBOL, but the character doesn't exist on your keyboard. You could assign the hexadecimal representation of the character () with the EVAL command:

```
EVAL SYMBOL = X'5F'
```

The ILE debugger is great, but the source-level function isn't available to you automatically. First, you must remember to create your ILE modules with the correct debug view.

SUMMARY

Although the ILE source debugger doesn't have all the features of some debuggers, it's a vast improvement over what we had. The AS/400 finally has a debugger that can help programmers debug programs in an intuitive fashion.

One function we would like to see in the ILE source debugger is the ability to watch a variable. This function would allow the constant and dynamic display of selected variable values as you step through the program. With source debuggers on a PC, this watch function usually occurs through a window. Another feature we would like to see is the ability to evoke a program when the debugger is started.

Chapter 13

Activation Groups

This chapter concentrates on the ILE feature of activation groups. An activation group is not specific to any ILE language. As such, the material in this chapter is, for the most part, ILE language-independent and only addresses specific languages to show how they may achieve a particular ILE behavior.

This chapter starts by introducing you to what an activation group is, and then shows you how activation groups are used. You'll learn about the benefits activation groups bring to OS/400; that is, resource isolation and performance considerations.

The concept of activation groups is probably the most critical to learn in ILE, and probably one of the hardest to understand. Think of activation groups as a box. A box can contain various items, whereas an ILE activation group contains resources.

Even though an activation group is not a physical item, it still has certain characteristics that are defined by the resources it *owns*. More precisely, an activation group is used to own resources for an ILE application. A few of the resources that are owned by an activation group are program-static and automatic variables, heaps, Open Data Paths (ODPs), and "commit scope." The concept is that all programs that are activated within an activation group are developed as one cooperative application. Given that these resources are all scoped to an activation group in ILE, this allows for optional isolation of applications, with the results described below.

♦ Much larger amounts of storage can be made available to an application. (This is possible because ILE activation groups have far greater storage available to them than OPM applications; and multiple activation groups can exist in an application, each with their own storage allocation.)

♦ Independent file sharing (when sharing is limited to an activation group).

♦ Independent commitment control (within the activation group).

♦ Isolated error handling within an application (based on activation group boundaries).

♦ Addressing protection.

CREATING ACTIVATION GROUPS

Now that you have a general idea of what is owned by activation groups, the next logical questions are, "How are activation groups created, and what is the correspondence between activation groups and programs?" An active activation group can contain running programs and service programs.

Going back to the box analogy, think of an active activation group as an open box that has some items inside. An activation group is not a physical object on the system like a program, but rather is created (activated) when a program is run. The determination of which activation group a program is activated into is made at the program creation step. The ACTGRP parameter of the Create Program (CRTPGM) command allows you to specify *NEW, *CALLER, or the name of an activation group.

Although you specify the activation group on the CRTPGM command, the activation group is not created until the program is called.

Figure 13.1 illustrates calling a program that was created with ACTGRP(*NEW). The system always creates a new activation group when the program is called, and cleans up the activation group when the program is finished. Note that the system generates a name for the activation group that is created. In this example, the system-generated name for the activation group is 1579234.

Figure 13.2 shows what happens when a program is created with ACTGRP set to a given name. As illustrated in step 3, the first time program ORDERENTRY is called, the activation group ORDENT is created, and all static storage is allocated and initialized. Step 5 shows what happens the second time ORDERENTRY is called from the same job. In this case, the activation group ORDENT already exists, so no activation group is created, and the program ORDERENTRY reattaches to the activation group ORDENT.

Figure 13.1: Using a *NEW Activation Group

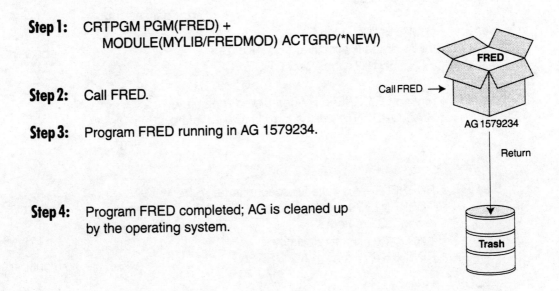

Step 1: CRTPGM PGM(FRED) +
              MODULE(MYLIB/FREDMOD) ACTGRP(*NEW)

Step 2: Call FRED.

Step 3: Program FRED running in AG 1579234.

Step 4: Program FRED completed; AG is cleaned up by the operating system.

Notice that no static initialization is done the second time ORDERENTRY is called. Calling a program the second time when it is in a named activation group is similar in notion to calling an OPM RPG program a second time when you don't set on the LR indicator in the previous invocation. The above is true for most ILE languages. ILE RPG, however, is the one exception. If you are entering a named activation group for the second time in ILE RPG and the first call ended with LR on, then the RPG program does the static initialization. This is deviating from one of the intents of a named activation group in ILE, but ILE RPG must retain compatibility with earlier versions of RPG for the case when the LR indicator was set on in the previous invocation.

Figure 13.3 illustrates calling a program that was created with ACTGRP *CALLER. In this example, the program INVENTORY is created with ACTGRP *CALLER. When INVENTORY is called from program ORDERENTRY (from the previous example), it runs in activation group ORDENT. When program INVENTORY is finished running, activation group ORDENT continues to exist with program ORDERENTRY still running in it, even though INVENTORY is no longer active.

Figure 13.2: Using a Named Activation Group

Step 1: CRTPGM PGM(ORDERENTRY) +
MODULE(MYLIB/ORDERMOD) ACTGRP(ORDENT)

Step 2: Call ORDERENTRY.

Step 3: AG ORDENT created.
Static storage is allocated and initialized.
ORDERENTRY runs in AG ORDENT.

Step 4: Program ORDERENTRY completed running,
but AG ORDENT remains in a "last-used" state.

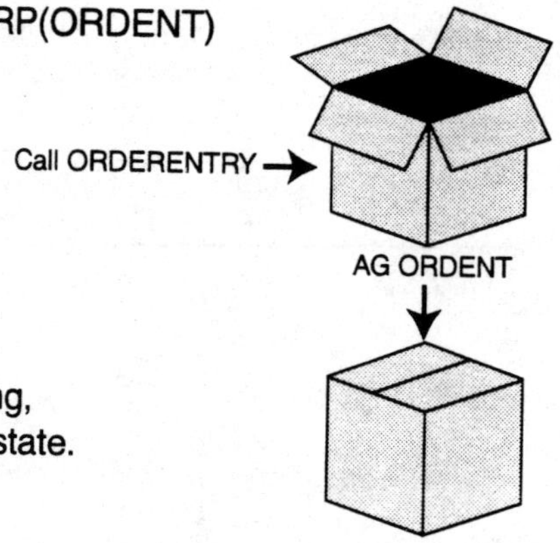

Step 5: ORDERENTRY is called a second time.
ORDERENTRY reattaches to AG ORDENT
(no new AG created).
Static storage is *not* reinitialized.
ORDERENTRY runs in AG ORDENT.

Call ORDERENTRY →

AG ORDENT

Call ORDERENTRY →

AG ORDENT

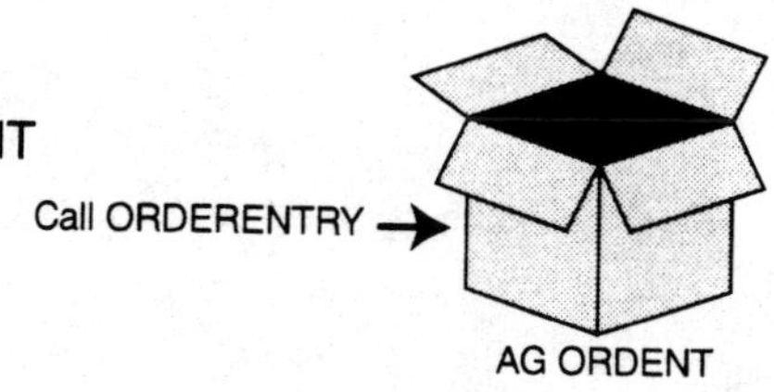

The ACTGRP parameter is also available on the Create Service Program (CRTSRVPGM) command. The valid values are *CALLER or the name of an activation group.

Notice that *NEW is not an option. The *CALLER and name values function in the same fashion as on the ACTGRP parameter on the CRTPGM command.

TERMINATING ACTIVATION GROUPS

Now that you know how activation groups are created, we need to talk about how activation groups are destroyed. But first, we'll discuss the concept of a control boundary. A control boundary is a call-stack entry that exists within your application whenever you call between activation groups.

Figure 13.3: Using a *CALLER Activation Group

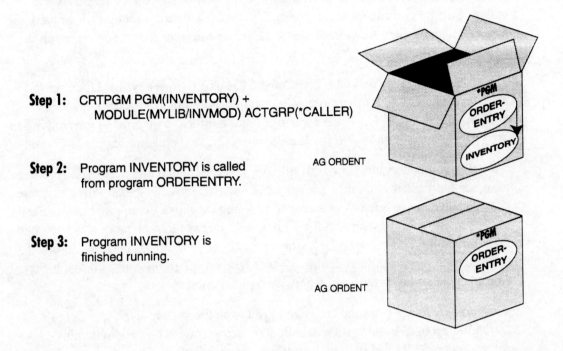

Step 1: CRTPGM PGM(INVENTORY) +
            MODULE(MYLIB/INVMOD) ACTGRP(*CALLER)

Step 2: Program INVENTORY is called
            from program ORDERENTRY.

Step 3: Program INVENTORY is
            finished running.

AG ORDENT

To be a little more precise, a control boundary is either an ILE call-stack entry whose immediately preceding call-stack entry is in a different activation group, or an ILE call-stack entry whose immediately preceding call-stack entry is an OPM program. These definitions are a little dry, but, later in this chapter, various examples are given to illustrate how control boundaries work. Now that control boundaries are out of the way, we can move on to terminating activation groups.

In order to understand how activation groups are terminated, it is best to classify the ways that you can leave an activation group. The two forms of leaving an activation group are a *soft leave* and a *hard leave*. Soft leaves have the characteristic that they return to the immediate caller and the activation group is left intact, leaving files open, and static storage for all program variables in a last-used state.

Hard leaves are classified as either normal or abnormal hard leaves. The characteristic of a hard leave is that it cancels call-stack entries until it reaches a control boundary.

If the control boundary is the first one in an ILE activation group, then the activation group is destroyed. After the activation group is destroyed, control returns to the caller of the destroyed activation group. Before the activation group is destroyed, the activation group files are closed; OS/400 frees up the storage and does an implicit commit or rollback.

You can use the ILE APIs CEETREC and CEE4ABN from any ILE language to achieve a hard leave. Furthermore, when an unhandled function check reaches a control boundary, it follows the same rules as a hard leave in terms of terminating the activation group. With regard to cleanup, however, the semantics can be different.

Now that you understand how activation groups are created and destroyed, you need to understand where activation groups exist—within jobs. As the previous examples show, you can have one or more activation groups within a given job, but you cannot share activation groups across jobs. This should be easy to remember if we go back to the box analogy. If you consider a storage locker to be a job, then it is easy to remember that you can have multiple boxes (activation groups) in a storage locker (job), but you cannot share a box between storage lockers.

There are always two special activation groups on the system—the user default activation group and the system default activation group. The system default activation group is used only by operating system functions.

The more interesting activation group is the user default activation group (DAG). There are a few things that make the DAG special. First, every job has a DAG. Second, all OPM programs run in the DAG.

You may not have realized that in V2R3 all RPG programs ran in the DAG. This means that OPM applications actually are running under ILE. It is the special characteristics of the DAG that enable OPM programs to run under ILE and still keep the same behavior they had prior to V2R3. Another special characteristic is that you can not delete the DAG. The DAG can only be deleted by the operating system when your job ends.

Performance Considerations

It is very important from a performance standpoint to realize that activation group creation is not very fast. Once again drawing an analogy to a box, it is much faster to put items into a box that is already created than to have to take cardboard, fold it, cut it, and tape it to create a box. In the same way, an activation group takes time to start off before the application starts running. If you reattach to an activation group that is already running, then you can start the application almost immediately.

Reattaching to an activation group is possible when using either *CALLER or a named activation group. Figure 13.4 shows two possible ways to set up an application. Method one has program MAINPGM running in an activation group called ONE. Each service program from which MAINPGM is calling functions is running in its own named activation group. Method two has program MAINPGM running in an activation group called ONE, and has all of the service programs running in *CALLER. Thus, all the service programs are activated into activation group ONE. Method one has better isolation of resources, but has far poorer startup performance than method two.

To further illustrate the benefits of understanding activation groups from a performance standpoint, Table 13.1 cites some performance figures for calling an RPG program (or procedure) a large number of times. These performance numbers were obtained on a dedicated system on a V3R1 system and will not necessarily be achieved in any given AS/400 environment. This data is presented only to give you a rough idea of how important it is to understand activation groups and the major benefits you can attain by using activation groups effectively.

Table 13.1: Calling Times for an Empty ILE RPG

Call Type	OPM	ILE (DAG)	ILE (Named AG)	ILE (*NEW AG)
CALL (LR ON)	121.6	90.5	7.2	4744.6
CALL (LR OFF)	5.7	4.7	4.8	4744.6
CALLB (LR ON)	N/A	2.7 (*CALLER)	Similar to ILE (DAG)	N/A
CALLB (LR OFF)	N/A	1.0 (*CALLER)	Similar to ILE (DAG)	N/A

The OPM numbers can be taken at face value, which shouldn't be a big surprise to RPG programmers. If the ILE RPG program is running in the DAG, the ILE numbers are better than OPM because there are some savings inherent in the initialization done by ILE RPG. You can see the huge performance benefit when calling a named activation group. The main reason for this performance increase is due to persistence. In other words, the resources you use stay around.

Figure 13.4: Two Methods of Setting Up Activation Groups

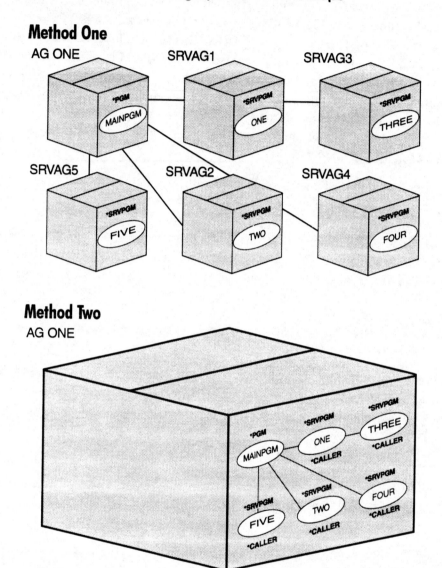

Given this, be aware that, if you call into a named activation group over and over again and use new resources each time, you may eventually run into resource (for example, storage) problems, because the amount of resources you are using would continue to grow. The incredibly high numbers for calling into a *NEW activation group are due to the time required to create and activate each *NEW activation group.

Notice that the difference between using LR on and LR off is lost when using a *NEW activation group. Finally, notice the improved times when using a CALLB (call bound) over a CALL (external call). The difference between a CALLB with LR off and a CALL with LR off is the difference in performance between an external call and a bound call. In the case of LR on, the CALLB case is faster because of the increased speed of a bound call and because no deactivation program is required.

Resource Scoping

The last thing discussed in this chapter is the scoping of resources. Resource scoping refers to how resources are shared and the locality of where the resources exist. The simplest resource to understand is the storage for your application. Storage for a program is scoped to an activation group.

Thus, if your application is made up of two activation groups, you have two isolated storage areas. Having two separate storage areas can protect sensitive data within an application from being damaged.

Separate storage areas also allow the application designer to break an application into separate logical entities whose data areas must only be accessible within each entity. For example, you may have an application that has an order-entry portion and a payroll portion. In this case, you would put the order-entry portion in one activation group and the payroll portion in another. This prevents any user of the order-entry system from being able to access the payroll data. Because of this isolation, we often refer to an activation group as a fire wall for resources.

Another type of resource scoping is data management scoping. There are many different types of data management resources, such as open file operations, overrides, commitment definitions, and local SQL cursors. Each data management resource has certain defining rules and default settings that dictate how they are scoped, be it at the call level, the activation-group level, or the job-scope level.

Let's take a look at a data management resource most RPG programmers are familiar with—overrides. Normally, the extent of a file override is to the call level, so that only programs running lower in the invocation stack are affected. Now, with ILE, you have far more flexibility in how you can control overrides. For example, the OVRDBF command has an option for the override scope called OVRSCOPE.

The possible choices for this option are *ACTGRPDFN, *CALLLVL, and *JOB. Obviously, *JOB means that there will be job-level scoping, and *CALLLVL means that there will be call-level scoping. The *ACTGRPDFN (Activation Group Defined) choice is a little more interesting. If you specify *ACTGRPDFN and the caller is in the DAG, then you get call-level scoping on the overrides. If you specify *ACTGRPDFN and the caller is not in the DAG, then the overrides are scoped to the activation group of the calling program.

As you can see, ILE gives you flexibility in terms of how you control the resources within your application. In ILE, you have the ability to control resources at a more granular level. More importantly, you can control resources at a more logical level. For example, you may want your order-entry application to have its resources separate from the rest of your application. This can easily be achieved by having the order-entry portion of your application run in its own activation group, and scoping the resources to the activation group.

The concepts in this chapter are summarized in Figure 13.5. As illustrated, activation groups are scoped to a JOB. Also demonstrated is the fact that there can be many activation groups within a JOB. Activation groups can have one or more programs or service programs running in them.

The three ways to specify which activation group a program or service program is activated into are *NEW, *CALLER, and name. If you want to have an ILE program run in the default activation group, then you must create the ILE program as *CALLER and call it from an OPM program, as illustrated for the DAG.

You can have multiple programs and service programs activated into a named activation group, as shown in the example for MYNAMEDAG. The activation group MYNAMEDAG also shows that a service program can be bound by reference to multiple different programs. Activation group 187526 shows that an activation group is created when you call a program that was created with ACTGRP(*NEW). It also shows that service programs can be activated into an activation group that was created as *NEW if the service program was created with ACTGRP(*CALLER). Lastly, as a review, ILE programs and service programs are created from one or more *MODULE objects.

By understanding ILE, and activation groups in particular, you will be able to design applications that have better performance, and you will have much better control of how your resources are used and protected within the application.

Figure 13.5: Activation Group Concepts Summary

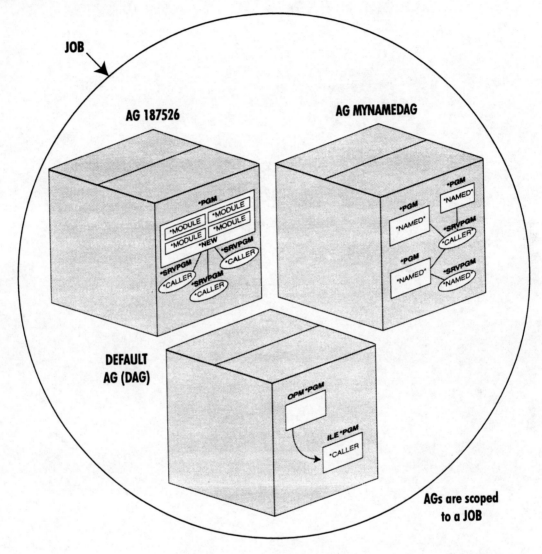

SUMMARY

Activation groups are substructures of a job and consist of system resources such as storage, commitment definitions, and open files. Activation groups make it possible for ILE programs running in the same job to run independently without intruding on each other. For example, you can perform commitment control and file overrides that apply to one group of programs within a job but not another. The basic idea is that all programs within an activation group are developed as one cooperative application.

Chapter 14

ILE RPG Exception Handling

In this chapter, you learn how ILE RPG handles program exceptions. ILE RPG offers the programmer more control over exception handling than RPG/400. The improved control allows your applications to be more tolerant of errors. In some cases, you may be able to recover from an error and allow the user to continue working in an application, eliminating abnormal termination of their work. For example, in RPG/400 there was no way to recover gracefully from a string operation that was outside a range of valid values. Even if you used a *PSSR subroutine, you were unable to return gracefully to the program statement that caused the exception. The best you could do was return to an RPG cycle point, such as *GETIN.

With ILE RPG, you have the ability to take some kind of action and continue processing at the very next statement beyond the statement that caused the error. You can eliminate user frustration caused by cryptic operating system messages interrupting their work. For example, there may be exceptions where you can simply take a default action and report the error to some kind of special application error log. Instead of being interrupted by a user stuck in an application, you and the user can continue being productive. To prevent interruptions, you cause the program to take a default action and/or log the exception to an error log for later review.

This chapter shows you how to use ILE to create your own customized error handling programs. A simple example is given to allow you to see how the new error handling methods can be integrated into your application programs.

WHAT IS AN EXCEPTION?

An exception is any run-time error that generates what is considered to be an exception condition or message. Two general types of run-time errors cause OS/400 to issue exception messages—*file exception/errors* and *program exception/errors*. An example of a file exception/error might be caused by trying to open a file already open, or an update operation prior to a read. As an example, a program exception/error might be caused by a *divide by zero*, or a reference to an out-of-range array subscript. (For a complete list of file and program exception/errors, see Appendix B.)

There are four possible types of exception messages:

*ESCAPE	An error causing a program to end abnormally, without completing its processing. After sending this message type, your program does not receive control.
*STATUS	Describes the status of work being done by the program. You may receive control after sending this message type. The way the receiving program handles the status message determines whether or not your program receives control.
*NOTIFY	Describes a condition requiring corrective action or a reply from the calling program. You may receive control after sending this message type. The way the receiving program handles the status message determines whether or not your program receives control.
Function Check	Describes an ending condition that has not been expected by the program and is not handled by an exception handler (for example, in CL, using the MONMSG command).

Exception messages are associated with call-stack entries. A call stack is a list of programs and procedures called by another program or procedure. For example, if program A calls program B, and program B calls procedure C, two programs are added to the call stack (A and B) and one procedure is added to the call stack (C). Programs and procedures are removed from a call stack in last-in-first-out (LIFO) order. When procedure C ends, it is removed from the call stack. When program B ends, it is removed from the call stack. Then, when program A ends, it is removed from the call stack.

If the call-stack entry is an ILE RPG program or procedure, there are four ways to handle the exception:

♦ An error indicator (indicator in columns 73 and 74 of the C-spec).

♦ A special file exception/error subroutine has been coded and defined through the INFSR keyword in an F-spec or a special program exception/error subroutine named *PSSR has been coded.

♦ A default exception handler (invoked if no error indicator or error subroutine was coded).

♦ A specific ILE condition handler.

The first three methods were available in RPG/400, but failed to provide the control most programmers really wanted or needed. The ILE condition handler method, however, is everything the RPG/400 programmer could hope for. With the ability to intercept errors with your own condition handler program, programmers can finally gain real control over exceptions. In the next section, you'll learn how to use ILE condition handlers to gain control of program errors.

ILE EXCEPTION PROCESSING

Each call-stack entry can be associated with a list of exception (condition) handlers defined for that entry. You can associate as many condition handler procedures with a program or procedure as you like. Associate ILE condition handlers with a program at run time by registering them with the Register ILE Condition Handler (CEEHDLR) bindable API. Example programs have been provided to illustrate how this is done.

If an exception is not handled, the following sequence of default actions is taken:

1. If the exception is a function check, the call-stack entry is removed.

2. The exception is moved (percolated) to the previous entry.

3.   The exception handling process is restarted for this call-stack entry.

The action of allowing the previous call-stack entry to handle an exception is referred to as percolation. Percolation continues until the exception is handled, or until a control boundary is reached. (A control boundary occurs at the initial program of an activation group or at an OPM program. In other words, a control boundary is a call-stack entry for which the immediately preceding call-stack entry is in a different control group or is an OPM program.)

In OPM, the exception message is associated with the program that is active. If the exception is not handled by any exception handlers, a function check is sent to the program that received the exception. If the function check isn't handled, then the program is removed from the stack and the function check is sent to the caller. The process repeats up the call stack (percolates) until the exception is handled.

In ILE, an exception message is associated with the procedure that is active on the call stack. If the exception is allowed to percolate, it is *not* converted to a function check. Each call stack is given a chance to handle the original exception until the control boundary is reached. At this point, the exception is converted to a function check and the exception processing starts all over again, beginning with the procedure that received the exception. This time, however, each call-stack entry is given a chance to handle the function check. If the control boundary is reached with the exception still unhandled, then a generic failure exception message (CEE9901) is sent to the caller of the procedure at the control boundary. Figure 14.1 illustrates this two-pass process.

In RPG/400, when an exception occurs and there's no specific handler enabled, an inquiry message is issued. In ILE RPG, this only happens if the exception is a function check. (A function check describes an ending condition that has not been expected by the program.) An ILE function check is a special message type that is sent only by the system. Under OPM, a function check is an escape message type with a message ID of CPF9999. If the function is not a function check, then the exception is passed to the caller of the procedure or program, and any eligible higher call-stack entries are given a chance to handle the exception. The following example illustrates the differences:

1.   Program A calls program B, which in turn calls program C.

2.   Program B has an error indicator coded for the call to program C.

3.   Program C has no error indicator or *PSSR error subroutine.

4.   Program C triggers an error.

Figure 14.1: Call Stack and Exception Message Percolation

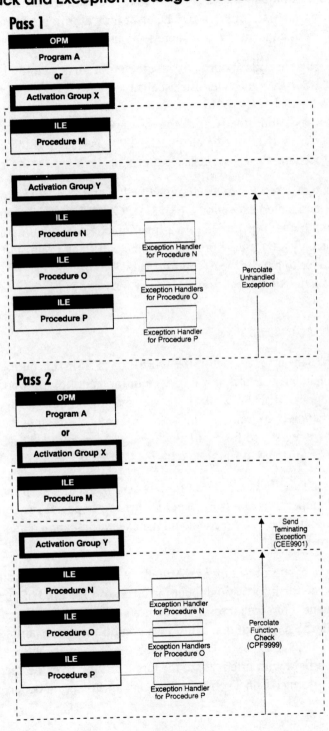

In RPG/400, an inquiry message is issued to program C. In ILE RPG, the exception is passed (percolated) to program B. The error indicator in program B is turned on, program C ends abnormally, and there is no inquiry message.

If an ILE program ends abnormally and the program is running in a different activation group than its caller, the escape message CEE9901 is issued and control is returned to the caller. If the ILE program is running in the same activation group as its caller and it ends abnormally, then the message issued depends on why the program ends. If it ends with a function check, CPF9999 is issued. If the exception is issued by an RPG procedure, the message has a prefix of RNX.

So, the main difference between how RPG/400 and ILE RPG process exceptions is in the area of unhandled exceptions. In ILE RPG, a program is given a chance to handle an exception before it is turned into a function check and an inquiry message is issued. It is only after all the programs in the call stack of an activation group are given a chance to handle the exception, but none of them handle it, that the message is turned into a function check and an inquiry message is issued.

ILE Condition Handlers

In addition to the error indicator, the INFSR or *PSSR subroutine, and the default exception handler, ILE offers specific condition handling support. Through condition handler programs, ILE RPG gives you a chance to explicitly handle exceptions. Condition handler programs are invoked instead of the default exception handler when they are registered for a call-stack entry. As mentioned earlier, condition handlers are registered at run time with the CEEHDLR bindable API.

If a condition handler is registered for a program and an exception occurs, the condition handler program is invoked. By setting a special variable in your condition handler program, the system considers the exception handled and your program can continue processing.

You want the condition handler program to at least log the error in some way. For example, write the information about the error to some kind of error log file or message queue. For some errors, you could take appropriate default action and resume after the statement that caused the conditions. For example, if a string operation created an exception, you could move a special sentinel value (for example, fill the result field with asterisks) to the target string. With the special value, the program is informed—in a soft manner—that an exception occurred.

If there is more than one condition handler for a call-stack entry and an exception occurs, the condition handler programs associated with the call-stack entry are given a chance to handle the exception in a LIFO order. (The last condition handler to be registered is the first program called, the first condition handler registered is the last program called.)

ILE CONDITION HANDLING EXAMPLE

The following programs illustrate how to code and register condition handler procedures. A simple example application is used where a program causes two exceptions that are handled by user-written condition handlers. There are three modules in this application: ILE1401R, ILE1491R, and ILE1492R (see Figures 14.2, 14.3, and 14.4).

Figure 14.2: Program ILE1401R

```
...+... 1 ...+... 2 ...+... 3 ...+... 4 ...+... 5 ...+... 6 ...+... 7
     D pConHdlr         S              *   PROCPTR
     D pConHdlr1        S              *   PROCPTR
     D                                     INZ(%paddr('ILE1491R'))

     D pConHdlr2        S              *   PROCPTR
     D                                     INZ(%paddr('ILE1492R'))

     D DSPsds          SDS                 NOOPT
     D   ProcName           *PROC
     Dzero              S              5  0 inz(0)
     Deleven            S              5  0 inz(11)
     Dresult            S              5  0
     Dneg1              S              3  0 inz(-1)
     Dstrng             S              5
     Darr               S              5    dim(10)

     C                   EVAL      pConHdlr = pConhdlr2
     C                   EXSR      RegHndlr

     C                   EVAL      pConHdlr = pConhdlr1
     C                   EXSR      RegHndlr

      * This exception handled by error handler procedure ILE1491R
     C                   EVAL      %SUBST(strng:neg1:3) = 'ABC'

      * This exception handled by error handler procedure ILE1492R
     C     10            DIV       zero          result
```

```
C                    EVAL      pConHdlr = pConhdlr1
C                    EXSR      DeRegHndlr

C                    EVAL      pConHdlr = pConhdlr2
C                    EXSR      DeRegHndlr

C                    EVAL      *inlr = *on
 *=============================================================
C     RegHndlr       BEGSR

C                    CALLB     'CEEHDLR'
C                    PARM                    pConHdlr
C                    PARM                    ProcName
C                    PARM                    *OMIT

C                    ENDSR
 *=============================================================
C     DeRegHndlr     BEGSR

C                    CALLB     'CEEHDLU'
C                    PARM                    pConHdlr
C                    PARM                    *OMIT

C                    ENDSR
 *=============================================================
C     *PSSR          BEGSR

C     'In *PSSR'     DSPLY
C     'Cancelling'   DSPLY

C                    ENDSR     '*CANCL'
 *=============================================================
...+... 1 ...+... 2 ...+... 3 ...+... 4 ...+... 5 ...+... 6 ...+... 7
```

Figure 14.3: Program ILE1491R

```
...+... 1 ...+... 2 ...+... 3 ...+... 4 ...+... 5 ...+... 6 ...+... 7
D CondTok         DS
D  MsgSev                       4B 0
D  MsgNo                        2A
D                               1A
D  MsgPrefix                    3A
D                               4A
D ProcName        S            10A

D Action          S             9B 0
 *
```

```
      * Action codes are:
      *
    D Resume          C                        10
    D Percolate       C                        20

    C      *ENTRY     PLIST
    C                 PARM                      CondTok
    C                 PARM                      ProcName
    C                 PARM                      action

    C                 IF          MsgPrefix = 'RNX' AND
    C                             MsgNo     = X'0100'
      * Out-of-range string operation exception handled
    C      'ORS Handled' DSPLY
    C                 EVAL        Action = Resume
    C                 ELSE
      * Unhandled, percolate exception
    C      'Percolating' DSPLY
    C                 EVAL        Action = Percolate
    C                 ENDIF
    C                 RETURN
    ...+... 1 ...+... 2 ...+... 3 ...+... 4 ...+... 5 ...+... 6 ...+... 7
```

Figure 14.4: Program ILE1492R

```
    ...+... 1 ...+... 2 ...+... 3 ...+... 4 ...+... 5 ...+... 6 ...+... 7
    D CondTok         DS
    D  MsgSev                          4B 0
    D  MsgNo                           2A
    D                                  1A
    D  MsgPrefix                       3A
    D                                  4A
    D ProcName        S               10A

    D Action          S                9B 0
      *
      * Action codes are:
      *
    D Resume          C                        10
    D Percolate       C                        20

    C      *ENTRY     PLIST
    C                 PARM                      CondTok
    C                 PARM                      ProcName
    C                 PARM                      action

    C                 IF          MsgPrefix = 'RNX' AND
    C                             MsgNo     = X'0102'
      * Handled divide by zero exception
```

```
C        'DBZ Handled' DSPLY
C                      EVAL      Action = Resume
C                      ELSE
  * Unhandled, percolate exception
C        'Percolating' DSPLY
C                      EVAL      Action = Percolate
C                      ENDIF
C                      RETURN
...+... 1 ...+... 2 ...+... 3 ...+... 4 ...+... 5 ...+... 6 ...+... 7
```

Program ILE1401R causes two exception errors to occur. The first is a substring error (caused by a value out of range for the string operation), and the second is a divide by zero. The substring exception/error is handled by condition handler procedure ILE1491R and the divide-by-zero exception/error is handled by a condition handler procedure ILE1492R. Because each exception/error program in this example only handles one error, and you can only have one procedure in an RPG program, separate programs are used for each exception/error.

The first thing program ILE1401R does is register the condition handler programs with the register handler API program CEEHDLR. ILE1492R is registered first and ILE1491R is registered second. Although condition handler programs can be registered in any order, ILE1492R was registered first in this example because the substring error in program ILE1401R is encountered first. Condition handler programs are processed in a LIFO order, so registering ILE1491R last allows the substring error to be handled first. When there is more than one condition handler program, and an exception is handled by one of the programs in the group, the remaining condition handler programs need not be processed. In this application, a substring error occurs and ILE1491R handles it. Because ILE1491R handles the exception, ILE1492R isn't called.

The divide-by-zero error occurs second. ILE1491R is called, but doesn't handle the error. So, the next condition handler (ILE1492R) is processed. ILE1492R is programmed to handle a divide-by-zero error (RNX0102), so it handles the message.

What really causes the system to consider an exception message to be handled is a variable that is passed to the CEEHDLR bindable API. The condition handler program simply sets the variable to a value that causes the API to recognize the exception as handled. You can see this variable in both ILE1491R and ILE1492R coded as the variable Action. You can see that Action is used as a parameter in the entry parameter list. You can also see that a certain message will cause the value 10, contained in the Resume variable, to be assigned to Action. In ILE1492R, the message prefix RNX and message number 0100 cause Action to be equal to Resume;

in ILE1492R, the message prefix RNX and message number 0102 cause Action to be equal to Resume. When the message prefix and number don't equate to the specific values coded in ILE1491R or ILE1492R, Action is set to the value (20) contained in the Resume variable. When Action equals 20, the exception message percolates to the previous call-stack entry.

Figure 14.5 shows the job log for the execution of ILE1401R. As you can see, the out-of-range string exception is handled first. Next the divide-by-zero exception occurs. ILE1491R attempts to handle it, but doesn't. Therefore, the "Percolated" message is displayed. ILE1492R is then processed and handles the divide-by-zero operation.

Figure 14.5: Job Log for Example of Handled Exceptions

```
                              Display All Messages
                                                      System:    MCPGMR
  Job . . :   QPADEV0003   User . . :    SHARIC     Number . . . :    064547


   > call tstileexp
     Value used is out of range for the string operation.
     DSPLY  ORS Handled
     Attempt to divide by zero.
     DSPLY  Percolating
     DSPLY  DBZ Handled
  >> dspjoblog




                                                                      Bottom
  Press Enter to continue.

  F3=Exit    F5=Refresh    F12=Cancel    F17=Top    F18=Bottom
```

SUMMARY

By now you see that ILE RPG brings a lot more power to the programmer when it comes to handling errors. Instead of allowing unexpected errors to cause you grief, you can plan for errors and control them as you choose.

Chapter 15

Pointers in ILE RPG

Among the many enhancements made to RPG in V3R1 is support for a new data type called a pointer. Pointers provide RPG programmers with an efficient new way to access data or code. While you probably won't use pointers in every application that you write, they can be extremely useful with certain types of low-level programming, such as retrieving data from a user space.

You may be familiar with the concept of pointers if you've used other programming languages such as C; but there are some slight differences in the implementation of pointers in RPG. In this chapter, we explain some of the concepts of pointers, discuss the RPG implementation, and show you an example of how to use them in an RPG application.

POINTER CONCEPTS

A pointer is a variable that contains the address of another variable. A pointer doesn't tell you what you'll find at an address location; it tells you only where to find it. For this reason, pointers are often referred to as *addresses*.

A simple analogy for a pointer is a street address. A street address doesn't tell you who lives in a particular house, but it does tell you where to find the house. Using the address, you can determine who lives there by going to the house and knocking on the door. Pointers work the same way. A pointer stores the address of a particular piece of data, so you can use that address to directly access the data at that address location. Pointers provide a convenient and efficient way to access data within your program.

Until ILE RPG, RPG hasn't had pointers, but OS/400 uses them extensively. One place in OS/400 where pointers are evident is in parameter passing. When parameters are passed between RPG or CL programs, they are actually passed by address, not by value. Have you ever accidentally coded a parameter with the wrong size in the receiving program and ended up with an unexpected value in an adjacent parameter? This happens when parameters are passed by address because the receiving program is expecting a larger field than was defined in the calling program. Parameters are passed by address, so you can easily corrupt your calling program data if the definition of the parameters are not the same in both programs.

Pointer Usage

The most likely candidates are programs that use the list APIs. The list APIs produce lists of data—such as fields, members, and objects—into a user space. Table 15.1 shows some common list APIs.

Table 15.1 Common List APIs

List API	Description
QSRLSAVF	List save files
QDCLCFGD	List configuration descriptions
QUSLMBR	List members
QDBLDBR	List database relations
QUSLFLD	List fields
QUSLRDCD	List record formats
QMHLJOBL	List job log messages
QMHLSTM	List non-program messages

List API	Description
QUSLOBJ	List objects
QPMLPRFD	List performance data
QBNLPGMI	List ILE program information
QBNLSPGM	List service program information
QSYLAUTU	List authorized users
QSYLATLO	List objects secured by authorization list
QSYLOBJP	List objects that adopt owner authority
QSYLOBJA	List objects user is authorized to
QSYLUSRA	List users authorized to object
QUSLSPL	List spooled files
QWCLASBS	List active subsystems
QUSLJOB	List jobs
QWCLSCDE	List job schedule entries
QWCLOBJL	List object locks
QWDLSJBQ	List subsystem job queues

Using pointers facilitates the process of extracting the list data out of the user space. Before we discuss how to extract data from a user space using pointers, let's first look at how the list APIs organize the data in a user space. Figure 15.1 shows the general layout of this type of data.

As you can see, the user space is broken down into four sections:

♦ Generic header

♦ Input parameter

- Header

- List data

Figure 15.1: Organization of User Space Data

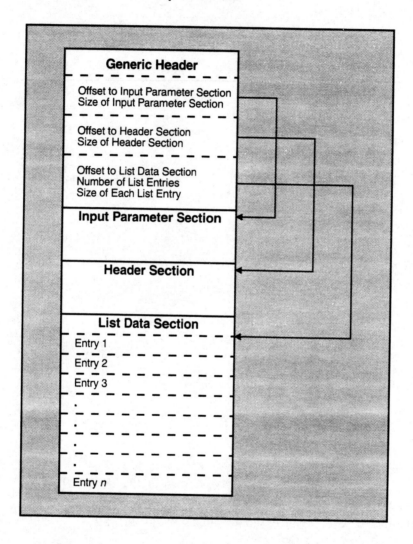

The generic header section is always found at the beginning of the user space and contains (among other things) the addresses of the other three sections. The input parameter section contains a copy of the parameters passed to the list API. This section is not usually needed and is, therefore, generally not extracted from the user space. The header section (not to be confused with the generic header) contains information related to the list. For example, the List Fields API places information such as the file type, record format, and record length in this section. The list data section is where the actual list is stored. This section is broken down into individual entries similar to records in a file.

Prior to the existence of pointers in RPG, the common technique to extract data from a user space was to call the Retrieve User Space (QUSRTVUS) API. This API needed to be called repeatedly to retrieve the individual sections of the user space as well as each entry in the list data section. The multiple external API calls slowed down the performance of the application. In addition, the Retrieve User Space API copied the data from the user space to a variable in the program.

RPG programs can now use pointers instead. Using pointers eliminates the need to perform repetitive external API calls and has the added benefit of being able to go to the memory location where the data exists and process it directly without having to first copy it into a variable.

An Example

Let's look at an example of an application that uses pointers. We chose the List Fields (QUSLFLD) API, but we could have chosen any list API to illustrate this technique. The List Fields API produces a list of fields from a database file and places them into a user space. In this example, we've written a command called List Fields (LSTFLD). This command accepts a database file as a parameter and produces a screen similar to the one shown in Figure 15.2. This screen lists the fields in the selected file along with their attributes and text.

The example consists of typical components of any utility application—a command (Figure 15.3), a CL program (Figure 15.4), a display file (Figure 15.5), and an ILE RPG program (Figure 15.6). The focus of this chapter is on pointers, so we'll discuss only the RPG program. We've supplied the other components so that you can use this application as a starting point for a similar application using one of the other list APIs.

Using pointers in an RPG program requires several pieces of code. The first is the data definition of the pointer, the second is a data structure or stand-alone field containing the BASED keyword, the third is a call to the Retrieve Pointer to User Space (QUSPTRUS) API, and the fourth is the use of the address (%ADDR) built-in function.

Figure 15.2: The List Fields Screen

```
                              List Fields

        File  . . . : ITEM01PF    Record format  . . : ITEMREC
        Library . . : DPSDS       File type  . . . . : PF

        Field        Len  Dec  Type   Text
        ITNUM          3    0    P     Item Number
        ITDESC        40         A     Item Description
        ITAMT          7    2    P     Item Amount
        ITLBFM         3    0    P     Label Format
        ITSTRQ         1         A     System Type Required Flag
        ITMDRQ         1         A     Media Required Flag
        ITRESC         1         A     Resource Library Flag
        ITCGRY         8         A     Item Category Code
        ITBDRT         5    5    P     Item Bad Debt Rate
        ITRTRT         5    5    P     Item Return Rate
        ITA#          12         A     Adjustment to Rev. GL #
        ITAL#         12         A     Allowance For Return GL #
        ITAR#         12         A     Accounts Receivable GL #
        ITBD#         12         A     Bad Debt Expense GL #
        ITCL#         12         A     Current Liability #

                                                       More...

        F3=Exit    F12=Cancel
```

Figure 15.3: The LSTFLD Command

```
/*================================================================*/
/* To compile:                                                    */
/*                                                                */
/*       CRTCMD     CMD(XXX/LSTFLD) PGM(XXX/FLD001CL) +           */
/*                  SRCFILE(XXX/QCMDSRC)                          */
/*                                                                */
/*================================================================*/
          CMD        PROMPT('List Fields')

          PARM       KWD(FILE) TYPE(QUAL) MIN(1) PROMPT('File')
          PARM       KWD(RCDFMT) TYPE(*NAME) DFT(*FIRST) +
                     SPCVAL((*FIRST)) PROMPT('Record format')

 QUAL:    QUAL       TYPE(*NAME) LEN(10)
          QUAL       TYPE(*NAME) LEN(10) DFT(*LIBL) +
                     SPCVAL((*LIBL)) PROMPT('Library')
```

Figure 15.4: CL Program FLD001CL

```
/*================================================================*/
/*                                                                */
/* To compile:                                                    */
/*                                                                */
/*        CRTCLPGM    PGM(XXX/FLD001CL) SRCFILE(XXX/QCLSRC)        */
/*                                                                */
/*================================================================*/
          PGM          PARM(&FILE &RCDFMT)

          DCL          VAR(&FILE) TYPE(*CHAR) LEN(20)
          DCL          VAR(&RCDFMT) TYPE(*CHAR) LEN(10)
          DCL          VAR(&MSGID) TYPE(*CHAR) LEN(7)
          DCL          VAR(&MSGDTA) TYPE(*CHAR) LEN(80)

          /* Send all errors to error handling routine */
          MONMSG       MSGID(CPF0000) EXEC(GOTO CMDLBL(ERROR))

          /* Create user space if necessary */
          CHKOBJ       OBJ(QTEMP/FLD001US) OBJTYPE(*USRSPC)
          MONMSG       MSGID(CPF9801) EXEC(CALL PGM(QUSCRTUS) +
                         PARM('FLD001US  QTEMP' ' ' 32767 ' ' +
                         '*ALL' 'User space for LSTFLD command'))

          /* Call the List Fields API */
          CALL         PGM(QUSLFLD) PARM('FLD001US  QTEMP' +
                         'FLDL0100' &FILE &RCDFMT '0')

          /* Call program to display fields */
          CALL         PGM(FLD001RG)

          /* Branch around error handling routine */
          GOTO         CMDLBL(ENDPGM)

          /* Error handling routine */
ERROR:    RCVMSG       MSGTYPE(*EXCP) MSGDTA(&MSGDTA) MSGID(&MSGID)
          SNDPGMMSG    MSGID(&MSGID) MSGF(QCPFMSG) MSGDTA(&MSGDTA) +
                         MSGTYPE(*ESCAPE)
ENDPGM:   ENDPGM
```

Figure 15.5: Display File FLD001DF

```
*================================================================
* To compile:
*
*        CRTDSPF    FILE(XXX/FLD001DF) SRCFILE(XXX/QDDSSRC)
*
*================================================================
```

```
*. 1 ...+... 2 ...+... 3 ...+... 4 ...+... 5 ...+... 6 ...+... 7
A                                         DSPSIZ(24 80 *DS3)
A                                         PRINT
A                                         CA03(03)
A                                         CA12(12)
A          R DSPSFL01                     SFL
A            FLDNAME       10A  O  7  2
A            FLDLENGTH      5Y 0O  7 13EDTCDE(3)
A            FLDDECPOS      3Y 0O  7 19EDTCDE(3)
A N60                                      DSPATR(ND)
A            DATATYPE       1   O  7 26
A            TEXT          50A  O  7 31
A          R DSPCTL01                     SFLCTL(DSPSFL01)
A                                         SFLSIZ(0016)
A                                         SFLPAG(0015)
A                                         OVERLAY
A                                         SFLDSP
A                                         SFLDSPCTL
A N03                                      SFLEND(*MORE)
A                                       1 35'List Fields'
A                                         DSPATR(HI)
A                                       3  2'File . . . :'
A            FILENAME      10A  O  3 16
A                                       3 29'Record format . . :'
A            RCDFORMAT     10A  O  3 50
A                                       4  2'Library . . :'
A            LIBRNAME      10A  O  4 16
A                                       4 29'File type . . . . :'
A            FILETYPE      10A  O  4 50
A                                       6  2'Field      Len'
A                                         DSPATR(HI)
A                                       6 20'Dec Type  Text'
A                                         DSPATR(HI)
A          R DSPRCD01
A                                      23  2'F3=Exit   F12=Cancel'
A                                         COLOR(BLU)
*. 1 ...+... 2 ...+... 3 ...+... 4 ...+... 5 ...+... 6 ...+... 7
```

Figure 15.6: RPG Program FLD001RG

```
*================================================================
* To compile:
*
*     CRTBNDRPG  PGM(XXX/FLD001RG) SRCFILE(XXX/QRPGLESRC)
*
*================================================================
*. 1 ...+... 2 ...+... 3 ...+... 4 ...+... 5 ...+... 6 ...+... 7 ...+... 8
FFLD001DF  CF   E             WORKSTN SFILE(DSPSFL01:Recno)

D SpacePtr        S               *
D HeaderPtr       S               *
```

```
*. 1 ...+... 2 ...+... 3 ...+... 4 ...+... 5 ...+... 6 ...+... 7 ...+... 8
D ListPtr          S                    *

D UserSpace        DS                       BASED(SpacePtr)
D  Data                           1         DIM(32767)
D  OffSetHdr             117    120B 0
D  OffSetLst             125    128B 0
D  NumLstEnt             133    136B 0
D  EntrySize             137    140B 0

D Header           DS                       BASED(HeaderPtr)
D  FileName                 1    10
D  LibrName                11    20
D  FileType                21    30
D  RcdFormat               31    40

D List             DS                       BASED(ListPtr)
D  FldName                  1    10
D  DataType                11    11
D  Length                  21    24B 0
D  Digits                  25    28B 0
D  DecPos                  29    32B 0
D  Text                    33    82

D SpaceName        S                   20   INZ('FLD001US  QTEMP')
D Recno            S                    5  0

 * Retrieve pointer to user space
C                   CALL       'QUSPTRUS'
C                   PARM                   SpaceName
C                   PARM                   SpacePtr


 * Get heading information
C                   EVAL       HeaderPtr = %ADDR(Data(OffSetHdr + 1))


 * Repeat for each entry in the List Data section
C                   DO         NumLstEnt


 * Get detail information
C                   EVAL       ListPtr = %ADDR(Data(OffSetLst + 1))


 * Load field Length and Decimal positions
C       .           IF         Digits = 0
C                   EVAL       FldLength = Length
C                   EVAL       *IN60 = *OFF
C                   ELSE
C                   EVAL       FldLength = Digits
C                   EVAL       FldDecPos = DecPos
C                   EVAL       *IN60 = *ON
C                   ENDIF
*. 1 ...+... 2 ...+... 3 ...+... 4 ...+... 5 ...+... 6 ...+... 7 ...+... 8
```

```
*. 1 ...+... 2 ...+... 3 ...+... 4 ...+... 5 ...+... 6 ..+... 7 ...+... 8
* Write subfile record
C                   EVAL      Recno = Recno + 1
C                   WRITE     DSPSFL01

* Get location of next entry
C                   EVAL      OffSetLst = OffSetLst + EntrySize

C                   ENDDO

* Write screen
C                   WRITE     DSPRCD01
C                   EXFMT     DSPCTL01

C                   EVAL      *INLR = *ON
*. 1 ...+... 2 ...+... 3 ...+... 4 ...+... 5 ...+... 6 ...+... 7 ...+... 8
```

In the following section of code, you can see the data definition of three pointers—SpacePtr, HeaderPtr, and ListPtr .

```
D SpacePtr        S               *
D HeaderPtr       S               *
D ListPtr         S               *
```

In ILE RPG, you define pointers by specifying an asterisk as the data type (position 40) on a data specification. In this example, we've coded these pointers as stand-alone fields as designated by the S in position 44. You can also code pointers as subfields of a data structure.

The following code shows three data structures: UserSpace, Header, and List.

```
D UserSpace       DS                        BASED(SpacePtr)
D  Data                           1         DIM(32767)
D  OffSetHdr            117     120B 0
D  OffSetLst            125     128B 0
D  NumLstEnt            133     136B 0
D  EntrySize            137     140B 0

D Header          DS                        BASED(HeaderPtr)
D  FileName              1      10
D  LibrName             11      20
D  FileType             21      30
D  RcdFormat            31      40

D List            DS                        BASED(ListPtr)
D  FldName               1      10
D  DataType             11      11
D  Length               21      24B 0
D  Digits               25      28B 0
D  DecPos               29      32B 0
D  Text                 33      82
```

All three data structures are based on a pointer variable that holds the address of an area of memory. In this case, the area of memory contains a portion of a user space. The BASED keyword provides the link. Notice that the data structure UserSpace is based on pointer variable SpacePtr, Header is based on HeaderPtr, and List is based on ListPtr. When a valid address is assigned to one of the pointer variables, the data structure based on the pointer variable overlays the data contained at that memory address. The data structure and its subfields can then be used to reference the data beginning at the location contained in the pointer variable. Before any of the fields in the data structure can be used, the basing pointer must be assigned a valid address; otherwise, an exception error is generated.

The following code shows the call to the Retrieve Pointer to User Space API.

```
C             CALL      'QUSPTRUS'
C             PARM                  SpaceName
C             PARM                  SpacePtr
```

This API has only two parameters—the name of a user space (SpaceName) and the name of a pointer (SpacePtr). After the call to this API, the pointer is set to the address of the beginning of the user space. This essentially overlays the data structure on top of the user space data because they both now begin at the same storage address. All of the subfields of data structure UserSpace are then available to the program. Among these subfields is the definition of a large array called Data, which is composed of single-byte elements. As you'll see, this array is used to retrieve the address of the other sections of the user space.

The following statement shows the use of the %ADDR built-in function:

```
C             EVAL      HeaderPtr = %ADDR(Data(OffSetHdr + 1))
```

This function retrieves the address of a storage location and places it into a pointer. Here, the function is used to retrieve the address of the beginning of the header section of the user space. The Data array is used to locate the beginning byte of the header section. That address is placed into the pointer called HeaderPtr. The Header data structure is based on this pointer, so all of the subfields become available. This overlays the Header data structure on top of the header section of the user space as they now share the same storage address. Because the value in OffSetHdr is a zero-based reference, it must be incremented by 1.

The program then drops into a loop to retrieve each of the entries in the list data section. During the first iteration, the following statement retrieves the address of the first element of the list data section:

```
C             EVAL      ListPtr = %ADDR(Data(OffSetLst + 1))
```

The Data array is used to locate the address of the beginning byte of the entry. That address is placed into the pointer called ListPtr (the based-on pointer for the List data structure). The List data structure now overlays the first entry in the list data section of the user space. Before the next iteration of the loop, the offset within the Data array is incremented by the size of the list entry with the following statement:

```
C                          EVAL      OffSetLst = OffSetLst + EntrySize
```

The new offset value allows the program to retrieve the address of the next entry. The loop is repeated until all of the entries in the list have been processed.

ONE FINAL POINT

As you've seen, pointers can be used effectively in ILE RPG to process data from a user space. This example could have been simplified, though, if IBM had taken a more traditional approach to pointer implementation in RPG. In other languages, such as C, it's common to simply increment a pointer to get to another storage location. Unfortunately, IBM doesn't allow pointer math in ILE RPG. This restriction is the reason for the large Data array in this example. By not allowing pointer math, it often becomes necessary to find alternative methods of retrieve address locations. Perhaps the next release of RPG will remove this limitation. Until then, this method is still a big improvement over the method we used prior to having pointers in RPG.

Appendix A

The Indent ILE RPG Utility

One of the problems with ILE RPG as a programming language is that it's still basically a fixed-format language. Although IBM has implemented some free-format operation codes, such as EVAL, IF, and DO, the language still prohibits the programmer from indenting code so that the reader can easily decipher the levels of structure being used.

INDENTING RPG SOURCE

In free-format languages such as BASIC, PL/I, or C, indenting code has never been a problem, and understanding code in these free-format languages is normally easier than reading RPG. To solve this problem, we created the Indent ILE RPG (INDILERPG) command. (You can download the source code for this utility from the MC-BBS. Use a modem and your favorite communications software.) While you still have to write in fixed format, it makes reading ILE RPG programs much easier.

To download this utility, use a modem to call MC-BBS at (619) 931-9909. Go to the Files area and select "Public Domain Files for AS/400." Download the files named INDILE.EXE. This is a self-extracting archive file containing the source code for this utility. To extract the utility, place this file in an empty subdirectory and execute it. Once the files are extracted, you need to upload the source code to the AS/400 using a file transfer facility such as those supplied with PC Support and Client Access.

Figure A.1 shows a sample of code in original form. Figure A.2 shows the same code after running it through the INDILERPG utility. By looking at these two figures, you can see how INDILERPG improves the readability of an ILE RPG program. This utility indents the ILE RPG code it finds between the structured operations IFxx, DO, DOWxx, DOUxx, SELECT/WHEN, and their corresponding END or ENDxx statements. It also draws vertical lines to show which portions of the program have been indented. The results can be viewed on the screen or sent to the printer.

Figure A.1: Regular ILE RPG Source Code

```
C                    READ      QRPGLESRC                             99
C                    DOW       *IN99 = *OFF AND SRCSEQ <= HISEQ
C                    IF        SRCSEQ >= LOWSEQ
C                    EXSR      CHKLVL
C                    EXSR      INDENT
C                    EXSR      WRTDTL
C                    END
C                    READ      QRPGLESRC                             99
C                    END
```

Figure A.2: Indented ILE RPG Source Code

```
C                    READ      QRPGLESRC
C                    DOW       *IN99 = *OFF AND SRCSEQ <= HISEQ
C                    | IF        SRCSEQ >= LOWSEQ
C                    | | EXSR      CHKLVL
C                    | | EXSR      INDENT
C                    | | EXSR      WRTDTL
C                    | END
C                    | READ      QRPGLESRC
C                    END
```

How INDILERPG Works

The prompt screen for the INDILERPG command is shown in Figure A.3.

The INDILERPG command has the following parameters:

♦ SRCMBR: Name of the source member containing the RPG source code to be indented. Normally, this is also the name of the program. This is the only mandatory parameter.

- ◆ SRCFILE: Qualified name of the source physical file where the source member resides. It defaults to QRPGLESRC in *LIBL.

- ◆ LOWSEQ: The beginning sequence number of the source member to start displaying or listing. The default is 0000.00.

- ◆ HISEQ: The ending sequence number of the source member to stop displaying or listing. The default is 9999.99.

- ◆ SYMBOL: The symbol you enter here is used by INDILERPG to join the beginning and ending of an indented block of code, such as an IFxx and its END. It defaults to a vertical bar. If your printer can't print a vertical bar, change it to some other character such as a colon, or even an opening parenthesis.

- ◆ COLUMNS: The number of columns to the right that INDILERPG should indent each level of code. You can enter any value between 1 and 5. The default value is 2.

- ◆ OUTPUT: Leave the default value of * to display the indented code, or change it to *PRINT to send it to the printer.

Figure A.3: The INDILERPG Command Prompt

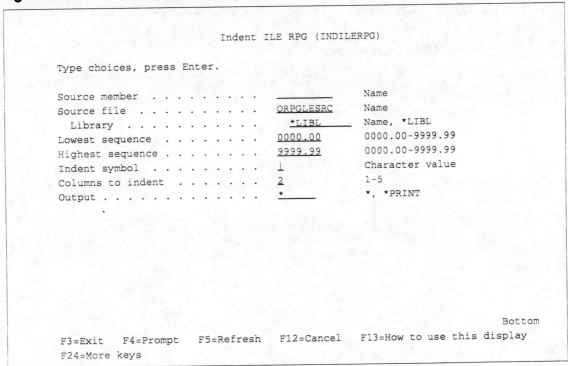

```
                        Indent ILE RPG (INDILERPG)

 Type choices, press Enter.

 Source member  . . . . . . . . .   _____     Name
 Source file  . . . . . . . . . .   QRPGLESRC      Name
   Library  . . . . . . . . . .       *LIBL        Name, *LIBL
 Lowest sequence  . . . . . . . .   0000.00        0000.00-9999.99
 Highest sequence . . . . . . . .   9999.99        0000.00-9999.99
 Indent symbol  . . . . . . . . .   |              Character value
 Columns to indent  . . . . . . .   2              1-5
 Output . . . . . . . . . . . . .   *____          *, *PRINT
       .



                                                              Bottom
 F3=Exit    F4=Prompt   F5=Refresh   F12=Cancel   F13=How to use this display
 F24=More keys
```

If OUTPUT(*PRINT) is specified, the command prompter asks for another parameter:

♦ PAGEBRK: Whether to break the listing into separate pages (each with a heading) when overflow occurs. The default is *NO, meaning that the printing is continuous, even over the perforation. This makes it easier to follow the indentations.

If you choose to view the output on the screen, you notice that the screen looks very much like SEU in browse mode. One difference is that there is a field on the screen labeled ROLL==>. The value in this field is the number of lines to roll when the Roll Up or Roll Down keys are pressed. The default is 20 lines, which is one full screen. You can increase or decrease this number to position the screen exactly where you want it. For example, try entering a 1 in this field and repeatedly press Roll Up. Notice that the screen scrolls very slowly. Entering 50 causes you to jump through the source code very quickly.

If you choose to print a listing, you notice that it looks very much like an SEU source listing. The difference here is that there is a column labeled IND USE. This column is used to show in which position you have coded resulting indicators. A 1, 2, or 3 in this column represents the corresponding indicator position. It is necessary on the indent listing because the indicators are shifted over when indented.

The code for the command, programs, display file, and printer file that make up INDILERPG are shown in Figures A.4 through A.8.

Figure A.4: The INDILERPG Command

```
/*================================================================*/
/* To compile:                                                    */
/*                                                                */
/*           CRTCMD     CMD(XXX/INDILERPG) PGM(XXX/RPG001RG) +    */
/*                      SRCFILE(XXX/QCMDSRC)                       */
/*                                                                */
/*================================================================*/
            CMD        PROMPT('Indent ILE RPG')

            PARM       KWD(SRCMBR) TYPE(*NAME) MIN(1) +
                         PROMPT('Source member')
            PARM       KWD(SRCFILE) TYPE(Q1) PROMPT('Source file')
            PARM       KWD(LOWSEQ) TYPE(*DEC) LEN(6 2) DFT(0000.00) +
                         RANGE(0000.00 9999.99) PROMPT('Lowest +
                         sequence')
            PARM       KWD(HISEQ) TYPE(*DEC) LEN(6 2) DFT(9999.99) +
                         RANGE(0000.00 9999.99) PROMPT('Highest +
                         sequence')
            PARM       KWD(SYMBOL) TYPE(*CHAR) LEN(1) DFT(|) +
```

```
                        PROMPT('Indent symbol')
            PARM        KWD(COLUMNS) TYPE(*DEC) LEN(1 0) DFT(2) +
                        RANGE(1 5) PROMPT('Columns to indent')
            PARM        KWD(OUTPUT) TYPE(*CHAR) LEN(6) RSTD(*YES) +
                        DFT(*) VALUES(* *PRINT) PROMPT('Output')
            PARM        KWD(PAGEBRK) TYPE(*CHAR) LEN(4) RSTD(*YES) +
                        DFT(*NO) VALUES(*YES *NO) PMTCTL(PC1) +
                        PROMPT('Break to new page on overflow')

PC1:        PMTCTL      CTL(OUTPUT) COND((*EQ *PRINT))

Q1:         QUAL        TYPE(*NAME) DFT(QRPGLESRC)
            QUAL        TYPE(*NAME) DFT(*LIBL) SPCVAL((*LIBL)) +
                        PROMPT('Library')
```

Figure A.5: The RPG001CL Program

```
/*================================================================*/
/*                                                                */
/* To compile:                                                    */
/*                                                                */
/*          CRTCLPGM  PGM(XXX/RPG001CL) SRCFILE(XXX/QCLSRC)       */
/*                                                                */
/*================================================================*/
PGM PARM(&SRCMBR &QSRCFILE &LOWSEQ &HISEQ &SYMBOL &COLUMNS +
    &OUTPUT &PAGEBRK)

DCL VAR(&COLUMNS)    TYPE(*DEC)  LEN(1 0)
DCL VAR(&FILE)       TYPE(*CHAR) LEN(10)
DCL VAR(&HISEQ)      TYPE(*DEC)  LEN(6 2)
DCL VAR(&LIB)        TYPE(*CHAR) LEN(10)
DCL VAR(&LOWSEQ)     TYPE(*DEC)  LEN(6 2)
DCL VAR(&MSGF)       TYPE(*CHAR) LEN(10)
DCL VAR(&MSGFLIB)    TYPE(*CHAR) LEN(10)
DCL VAR(&MSGDTA)     TYPE(*CHAR) LEN(132)
DCL VAR(&MSGID)      TYPE(*CHAR) LEN(7)
DCL VAR(&OUTPUT)     TYPE(*CHAR) LEN(6)
DCL VAR(&PAGEBRK)    TYPE(*CHAR) LEN(4)
DCL VAR(&QSRCFILE)   TYPE(*CHAR) LEN(20)
DCL VAR(&SRCF)       TYPE(*CHAR) LEN(21)
DCL VAR(&SRCMBR)     TYPE(*CHAR) LEN(10)
DCL VAR(&SYMBOL)     TYPE(*CHAR) LEN(1)

MONMSG MSGID(CPF0000) EXEC(GOTO CMDLBL(ERROR))

/* Break qualified name */
CHGVAR VAR(&FILE) VALUE(%SST(&QSRCFILE 1 10))
CHGVAR VAR(&LIB) VALUE(%SST(&QSRCFILE 11 10))
RTVMBRD FILE(&LIB/&FILE) MBR(&SRCMBR) RTNLIB(&LIB)

/* Override files as needed */
OVRDBF FILE(QRPGLESRC) TOFILE(&LIB/&FILE) MBR(&SRCMBR) LVLCHK(*NO)
```

```
    IF COND(&OUTPUT *EQ '*PRINT') THEN(OVRPRTF FILE(RPG001PR) +
        USRDTA(&SRCMBR))

    CHGVAR VAR(&SRCF) VALUE(&LIB *TCAT '/' *CAT &FILE)

    OVRPRTF FILE(RPG001PR) PRTTXT(*BLANK)
    CALL PGM(RPG001RG) PARM(&SRCMBR &SRCF &LOWSEQ &HISEQ &SYMBOL +
        &COLUMNS &OUTPUT &PAGEBRK)
    DLTOVR FILE(RPG001PR)

    GOTO CMDLBL(END)

    /* Send error message */
ERROR: +
    RCVMSG MSGTYPE(*EXCP) MSGDTA(&MSGDTA) MSGID(&MSGID) MSGF(&MSGF) +
        MSGFLIB(&MSGFLIB)
    SNDPGMMSG MSGID(&MSGID) MSGF(&MSGFLIB/&MSGF) MSGDTA(&MSGDTA) +
        MSGTYPE(*ESCAPE)

    /* End program */
END: +
    ENDPGM
```

Figure A.6: The RPG001RG Program

```
    *================================================================
    * To compile:
    *
    *      CRTBNDRPG  PGM(XXX/ILE001RG) SRCFILE(XXX/QRPGLESRC)
    *
    *================================================================
    *. 1 ...+... 2 ...+... 3 ...+... 4 ...+... 5 ...+... 6 ...+... 7
    FQRPGLESRC IF   F  112        DISK
    FILE001PR  O    E             PRINTER OFLIND(*IN01)
    F                                     USROPN
    FILE001DF  CF   E             WORKSTN USROPN
    F                                     SFILE(SFLREC:SFLRRN)


    D LIN           S              1    DIM(105)
    D BAR           S             71    DIM(2) CTDATA PERRCD(1)

    D               DS
    D  INDUSE                      1      5
    D  USE1                        1      1
    D  USE2                        3      3
    D  USE3                        5      5
    D               DS
    D  SEQNBR                      1      7
    *. 1 ...+... 2 ...+... 3 ...+... 4 ...+... 5 ...+... 6 ...+... 7
```

```
*. 1 ...+... 2 ...+... 3 ...+... 4 ...+... 5 ...+... 6 ...+... 7
D   SEQNM1                        1     4
D   DECPNT                        5     5
D   SEQNM2                        6     7


IQRPGLESRC NS
I                                        1     6 2SRCSEQ
I                                        7    12 0SRCDAT
I                                       13   112  SRCDTA
I                                       20   112  COMENT
I                                       18    18  SPEC
I                                       19    19  ASTRSK
I                                       13    19  COMSPC
I                                       13    15  ARRAYS
I                                       38    39  OPCD2
I                                       38    40  OPCD3
I                                       38    42  OPCD5
I                                       13    37  LSRC
I                                       38   112  RSRC
I                                       83    84  IND1
I                                       85    86  IND2
I                                       87    88  IND3
 *****************************************************************
C     *ENTRY        PLIST
C                   PARM                      MBR      10
C                   PARM                      SRCF     21
C                   PARM                      LOWSEQ    6 2
C                   PARM                      HISEQ     6 2
C                   PARM                      SYMBOL    1
C                   PARM                      COLS      1 0
C                   PARM                      OUTPUT    6
C                   PARM                      PAGBRK    4


C                   EXSR        WRTHDR

C                   READ        QRPGLESRC                          99
C                   DOW         *IN99 = *OFF AND SRCSEQ <= HISEQ
C                   IF          SRCSEQ >= LOWSEQ
C                   EXSR        CHKLVL
C                   EXSR        INDENT
C                   EXSR        WRTDTL
C                   END
C                   READ        QRPGLESRC                          99
C                   END

C                   EXSR        WRTFTR

C                   SETON                                          LR
 *****************************************************************
C     CHKLVL        BEGSR
 *. 1 ...+... 2 ...+... 3 ...+... 4 ...+... 5 ...+... 6 ...+... 7
```

```
 *. 1 ...+... 2 ...+... 3 ...+... 4 ...+... 5 ...+... 6 ...+... 7
C                   MOVEA     *BLANK         LIN
C                   MOVE      *BLANK         INDUSE

C                   IF        SHIFT = 'Y' AND OPCD3 <> 'AND'
C                             AND OPCD2 <> 'OR'
C                   ADD       1              LEVEL            3 0
C                   MOVE      *BLANK         SHIFT            1
C                   END

C                   IF        SPEC = 'C' AND ASTRSK <> '*' AND
C                             ASTRSK <> '/' AND ASTRSK <> '+'

C                   IF        OPCD2 = 'IF' OR OPCD2 = 'DO'
C                             OR OPCD2 = 'SELEC'
C                   MOVE      'Y'            SHIFT
C                   ELSE
C                   IF        OPCD3 = 'CAS'
C                   MOVE      'Y'            CASE             1
C                   ELSE
C                   IF        OPCD3 = 'END'
C                   IF        CASE <> 'Y'
C                   IF        LEVEL > *ZERO
C                   SUB       1              LEVEL
C                   ELSE
C                   Z-ADD     *ZERO          LEVEL
C                   END
C                   ELSE
C                   MOVE      *BLANK         CASE
C                   END
C                   END
C                   END
C                   END
C                   IF        IND1 <> *BLANKS
C                   MOVE      '1'            USE1
C                   END
C                   IF        IND2 <> *BLANKS
C                   MOVE      '2'            USE2
C                   END
C                   IF        IND3 <> *BLANKS
C                   MOVE      '3'            USE3
C                   END
C                   END
C                   ENDSR
 *****************************************************************
C     INDENT        BEGSR
C                   IF        LEVEL = *ZERO
C                   MOVEA     SRCDTA         LIN
C                   ELSE

 *. 1 ...+... 2 ...+... 3 ...+... 4 ...+... 5 ...+... 6 ...+... 7
```

```
*. 1 ...+... 2 ...+... 3 ...+... 4 ...+... 5 ...+... 6 ...+... 7
C                    MOVE     *BLANK          ELSE              1
C                    IF       ASTRSK <> '*' AND
C                             ASTRSK <> '/' AND
C                             ASTRSK <> '+'
C                    MOVEA    LSRC            LIN
C                    IF       OPCD5 = 'ELSE ' OR
C                             OPCD2 = 'WH' OR
C                             OPCD5 = 'OTHER'
C                    MOVE     'Y'             ELSE
C                    END
C                    END

C                    Z-ADD    26              X               3 0
C         1          DO       LEVEL           LVLNUM          3 0
C                    IF       ASTRSK = '*' OR
C                             ELSE <> 'Y' OR
C                             LVLNUM <> LEVEL
C                    IF       LVLNUM <= MAXLVL
C                    MOVEA    SYMBOL          LIN(X)
C                    ADD      COLS            X
C                    END
C                    END
C                    END

C                    IF       ASTRSK <> '*' AND
C                             ASTRSK <> '/' AND
C                             ASTRSK <> '+'
C                    MOVEA    RSRC            LIN(X)
C                    ELSE
C                    MOVEA    COMSPC          LIN
C                    MOVEA    COMENT          LIN(X)
C                    END
C                    END
C                    ENDSR
 ***************************************************************
C    WRTDTL          BEGSR
C                    IF       ARRAYS = '** '
C                    MOVE     'Y'             DATA              1
C                    END

C                    MOVEL    SRCSEQ          SEQNM1
C   .                MOVE     '.'             DECPNT
C                    MOVE     SRCSEQ          SEQNM2

C                    IF       OUTPUT = '*PRINT'
C                    MOVEA    LIN             PRTLIN
C                    MULT     100.0001        SRCDAT
C                    IF       PAGBRK = '*YES' AND *IN01 = *ON
C                    WRITE    HEADER
*. 1 ...+... 2 ...+... 3 ...+... 4 ...+... 5 ...+... 6 ...+... 7
```

```
      *. 1 ...+... 2 ...+... 3 ...+... 4 ...+... 5 ...+... 6 ...+... 7
C                     MOVE      '0'             *IN01
C                     END
C                     WRITE     DETAIL
C                     ELSE
C                     MOVEA     LIN             DSPLIN
C                     ADD       1               SFLRRN           4 0
C                     WRITE     SFLREC
C                     END
C                     ENDSR
      *****************************************************************
C     WRTHDR          BEGSR
C                     IF        OUTPUT = '*PRINT'
C                     WRITE     HEADER
C                     ELSE
C                     Z-ADD     20              ROLL
C                     MOVEL     BAR(1)          DSPLIN
C                     Z-ADD     1               SFLRRN
C                     WRITE     SFLREC
C                     END
C                     ENDSR
      *****************************************************************
C     WRTFTR          BEGSR
C                     IF        OUTPUT = '*PRINT'
C                     WRITE     FOOTER
C                     ELSE
C                     MOVE      *BLANK          SEQNBR
C                     MOVEL     BAR(2)          DSPLIN
C                     ADD       1               SFLRRN
C                     WRITE     SFLREC
C                     EXFMT     CTLREC
C                     END
C                     ENDSR
      *****************************************************************
C     *INZSR          BEGSR
C                     IF        OUTPUT = '*PRINT'
C                     OPEN      ILE001PR
C                     ELSE
C                     OPEN      ILE001DF
C                     END
C  40                 DIV       COLS            MAXLVL           2 0
C                     ENDSR
      *****************************************************************
**

*************** Beginning of data *********************************
*************** End of data ***************************************
```

Figure A.7: The RPG001DF Display File

```
*=================================================================
* To compile:
*
*      CRTDSPF    FILE(XXX/RPG001DF) SRCFILE(XXX/QDDSSRC)
*
*=================================================================
*. 1 ...+... 2 ...+... 3 ...+... 4 ...+... 5 ...+... 6 ...+... 7
A                                      DSPSIZ(24 80 *DS3)
A                                      PRINT
A                                      CA03(03 'EXIT')
A                                      CA12(12 'CANCEL')
 *
A          R SFLREC                    SFL
A            SEQNBR        7A  O  3  2
A            DSPLIN       71A  O  3 10
 *
A          R CTLREC                    SFLCTL(SFLREC)
A                                      SFLSIZ(0022)
A                                      SFLPAG(0021)
A                                      SFLDSP
A                                      SFLDSPCTL
A N80                                  SFLEND(*MORE)
A                                    1  2'Columns . . . :    1  71'
A                                    1 32'Indent RPG Source'
A                                      DSPATR(HI)
A            SRCF         21A  O  1 60
A                                    2  2'ROLL==>'
A            MBR          10A  O  2 60
A            ROLL          4  0B  2 10SFLROLVAL
*. 1 ...+... 2 ...+... 3 ...+... 4 ...+... 5 ...+... 6 ...+... 7
```

Figure A.8: The RPG001PR Printer File

```
*=================================================================
* To compile:
*
*      CRTPRTF    FILE(XXX/RPG001PR) SRCFILE(XXX/QDDSSRC)
*
*=================================================================
*. 1 ...+... 2 ...+... 3 ...+... 4 ...+... 5 ...+... 6 ...+... 7
A          R HEADER
A                                    1  1DATE
A                                       EDTCDE(Y)
A                                    1 12TIME
A                                    1 50'INDENT RPG SOURCE'
A                                    1125'PAGE'
A                                    1129PAGNBR
```

```
*. 1 ...+... 2 ...+... 3 ...+... 4 ...+... 5 ...+... 6 ...+... 7
A                                      EDTCDE(3)
A                                    3  1'SOURCE FILE . . . . . . .'
A             SRCF          21       3 28
A                                    4  1'MEMBER  . . . . . . . . .'
A             MBR           10       4 28
A                                    6  1'SEQ NBR'
A                                    6  9'*...+... 1 ...+... 2 ...+... -
A                                       3 ...+... 4 ...+... 5 ...+... -
A                                       6 ...+... 7 ...+... 8 ...+... -
A                                       9 ...+... 0'
A                                    6115'IND USE'
A                                    6125'CHG DATE'
A           R DETAIL                     SPACEB(1)
A             SEQNBR       7A        1
A             PRTLIN      105        9
A             INDUSE        5        116
A             SRCDAT        6  0     125EDTCDE(Y)
A           R FOOTER                     SPACEB(2)
A                                    38 '* * * *'
A                                    47 'E N D  O F  S O U R C E'
A                                    72 '* * * *'
*. 1 ...+... 2 ...+... 3 ...+... 4 ...+... 5 ...+... 6 ...+... 7
```

THE IBM VERSION

You may also decide to use the IBM version of ILE RPG indenting. Both the Create RPG Module (CRTRPGMOD) command and the Create Bound RPG Program (CRTBNDRPG) command allow you to create an indented compile listing. To use this feature, change the parameter INDENT from the default of *NONE to the indention symbol of your choice. This is a nice feature and shows that IBM agrees that indenting RPG code is a good idea. However, it has several disadvantages over the INDILERPG command. It requires that you compile the source in order to see it in its indented form—and you know how slow compiles can be. You may decide that the old method of drawing lines with a pencil is faster than waiting for a compile to finish.

With the IBM method, you can not display an indented listing without creating a spool file. INDILERPG gives you a choice of output device (screen or printer). INDILERPG allows you to display or print sections of the source member by using the LOWSEQ and HISEQ parameters. So, if you only need to work on part of the source member, such as a subroutine, you can display or print only those statements.

Give INDILERPG a try. We think you'll find that it will help you get up to speed on ILE RPG faster. And it's written in ILE RPG, so you'll learn some ILE RPG techniques as you look at the code.

Appendix B

ILE RPG Exception/Error Codes

The tables in this appendix contain exception/error codes that OS/400 returns to an ILE RPG program for program exception/errors and file exception/errors.

PROGRAM EXCEPTIONS

Program exception/errors are issued by OS/400 to ILE RPG when certain program errors occur (for example, divide by zero or invalid array index). Any code greater than 99 is considered an exception/error condition (Tables B.1 and B.2).

Table B.1: Program Exception Normal Codes

Code	Condition
00000	No exception/error occurred.
00001	Called program returned with the LR indicator on.

Table B.2: Program Exception/Error Codes

Code	Condition
00100	Value out of range for string operation.
00101	Negative square root.
00102	Divide by zero.
00103	An intermediate result is not large enough to contain the result.
00112	Invalid date, time, or time-stamp value.
00113	Date overflow or underflow. (For example, when the result of a Date calculation results in a number greater than *HIVAL or less than *LOVAL.)
00114	Date mapping errors, where a Date is mapped from a 4-character year to a 2-character year and the date range is not 1940 to 2039.
00120	Table or array out of sequence.
00121	Array index not valid.
00122	OCCUR outside of range.
00123	Reset attempted during initialization step of program.
00202	Called program or procedure failed; halt indicator (H1 through H9) not on.
00211	Error calling program or procedure.
00221	Called program tried to use a parameter not passed to it.
00222	Pointer or parameter error.
00231	Called program or procedure returned with halt indicator on.
00232	Halt indicator on in this program.
00233	Halt indicator on when RETURN operation run.
00299	RPG IV formatted dump failed.
00333	Error on DSPLY operation.

Code	Condition
00401	Data area specified on IN/OUT not found.
00402	*PDA not valid for non-prestart job.
00411	Data area type or length does not match.
00412	Data area not locked for output.
00413	Error on IN/OUT operation.
00414	User not authorized to use data area.
00415	User not authorized to change data area.
00421	Error on UNLOCK operation.
00431	Data area previously locked by another program.
00432	Data area locked by program in the same process.
00450	Character field not entirely enclosed by shift-out and shift-in characters.
00501	Failure to retrieve sort sequence.
00502	Failure to convert sort sequence.
00802	Commitment control not active.
00803	Rollback operation failed.
00804	Error occurred on COMMIT operation.
00805	Error occurred on ROLBK operation.
00907	Decimal data error (digit or sign not valid).
00970	The level number of the compiler used to generate the program does not agree with the level number of the RPG IV run-time subroutines.
09998	Internal failure in RPG IV compiler or in run-time subroutines.
09999	Program exception in system routine.

FILE EXCEPTIONS

OS/400 sends file exception/errors codes to ILE RPG when certain file exceptions occur (for example, an undefined record type is encountered or an I/O operation is executed against a closed file). Any code greater than 99 is considered an exception/error condition (Tables B.3 and B.4).

Table B.3: File Exception Normal Codes

Code	Device*	Condition
00000		No exception/error.
00002	W	Function key used to end display.
00011	W,D,SQ	End of file on a read (input).
00012	W,D,SQ	No-record-found condition on CHAIN, SETLL, and SETGT operations.
00013	W	Subfile is full on WRITE operation.

Table B.4: File Exception/Error Codes

Code	Device*	Condition
01011	W,D,SQ	Undefined record type (input record does not match record identifying indicator).
01021	W,D,SQ	Tried to write a record that already exists (file being used has unique keys and key is duplicate, or attempted to write duplicate relative record number to a subfile).
01022	D	Referential constraint error detected on file member.
01031	W,D,SQ	Match field out of sequence.
01041	N/A	Array/table load sequence error.
01042	N/A	Array/table load sequence error. Alternate collating sequence used.

Code	Device*	Condition
01051	N/A	Excess entries in array/table file.
01071	W,D,SQ	Numeric sequence error.
01121	W	No indicator on the DDS keyword for Print key.
01122	W	No indicator on the DDS keyword for Roll Up key.
01123	W	No indicator on the DDS keyword for Roll Down key.
01124	W	No indicator on the DDS keyword for Clear key.
01125	W	No indicator on the DDS keyword for Help key.
01126	W	No indicator on the DDS keyword for Home key.
01201	W	Record mismatch detected on input.
01211	All	I/O operation to a closed file.
01215	All	OPEN issued to a file already opened.
01216	All	Error on an implicit OPEN/CLOSE operation.
01217	All	Error on an explicit OPEN/CLOSE operation.
01218	D,SQ	Record already locked.
01221	D,SQ	Update operation attempted without a prior read.
01222	D,SQ	Record can not be allocated due to referential constraint error.
01231	SP	Error on SPECIAL file.
01235	P	Error in PRTCTL space or skip entries.
01241	D,SQ	Record number not found. (Record number specified in record address file is not present in file being processed.)
01251	W	Permanent I/O error occurred.

Code	Device*	Condition
01255	W	Session or device error occurred. Recovery may be possible.
01261	W	Attempt to exceed maximum number of acquired devices.
01271	W	Attempt to acquire unavailable device.
01281	W	Operation to unacquired device.
01282	W	Job ending with controlled option.
01284	W	Unable to acquire second device for single device file.
01285	W	Attempt to acquire a device already acquired.
01286	W	Attempt to open shared file with SAVDS or IND options.
01287	W	Response indicators overlap IND indicators.
01299	W,D,SQ	Other I/O error detected.
01331	W	Wait time exceeded for READ from WORKSTN file.

*Notes:

P = PRINTER
D = DISK
W = WORKSTN
SP = SPECIAL
SQ = Sequential

Index

D